THE
EIGHT
NEW RULES
OF REAL
ESTATE

DOING BUSINESS IN A CONSUMER-CENTRIC, TECHNO-SAVVY WORLD

John Tuccillo, Ph.D., CAE

Real Estate
Education Company®
a division of Dearborn Financial Publishing, Inc.

While a great deal of care has been taken to provide accurate and current information, the ideas, suggestions, general principles and conclusions presented in this text are subject to local, state and federal laws and regulations, court cases and any revisions of same. The reader is thus urged to consult legal counsel regarding any points of law—this publication should not be used as a substitute for competent legal advice.

Director, Product Development: Carol L. Luitjens
Executive Editor: Diana Faulhaber
Project Manager: Ronald J. Liszkowski
Art Manager: Lucy Jenkins

Printed in the United States of America

99 00 01 10 9 8 7 6 5 4 3

ISBN No.: 0-7931-3166-9

Tuccillo, John A.
    The eight new rules of real estate / by John Tuccillo.
       p.cm.
    Includes bibliographical references and index.
    ISBN 0-7931-3166-9
    1. Real estate business.   2. Real estate business—Data
processing.   3. Real estate business—Technological innovations.
4. Real estate management.   5. Real estate agents— Training of.
6. Real estate business—United States.   I. Title.
HD1375.T73   1999   98-39940
333.33—dc21   CIP

DEDICATION

This book is dedicated to the Research and Real Estate Finance staffs of the National Association of REALTORS®, 1987–1997. You guys never failed to make me look good, and you created as fine an operation as any trade association has ever seen.

CONTENTS

FOREWORD

John Tucillo is truly a remarkable thinker. Although schooled in Economics (Ph.D.) and matured in a national association structure, he steadfastly refuses to stay within any of the boundaries of thought this background would normally imply.

John has an uncanny ability to gather the right and meaningful facts and synthesize this data to determine and predict trends which will have dramatic effects on our industry. This alone requires a keen focus and a broad knowledge of the past, present, and future of our business. This however, is only the beginning of the process with John; he then reaches beyond his formal training and actually practically applies the knowledge to advise on business practices and plans.

John is a voracious reader, a consummate thinker, a nationally recognized economist, a sought after speaker, and a successful consultant in the industry. He gathers and analyses data in real time. By the time you finish reading this book, he will have new insights and new directions. This is just the beginning or benchmark for the survivor in the Residential Real Estate Business.

James F. Sherry
President & CEO
Interealty

New Rules?! New Rules?! I Didn't Even Know the Old Ones!

THE PACE OF CHANGE IS DIZZYING

In the movie "Airplane!," a crippled jetliner is guided (somewhat) safely to a landing in Chicago by a nervous ex-pilot who is a passenger on the plane. It lands without the benefit of tires and so skids along the runway to a stop. As it skids, those waiting in the terminal for the plane are advised that it's landing at Gate 4, then Gate 5, then Gate 6, etc. The result is they run frantically from gate to gate, never quite knowing when they will stop. The scene is funnier than I have described (which is why I'm not a screen-writer), but it resonates with the way many of us feel in this world of sudden, rapid, and unpredictable change.

We used to be able to predict the future by extrapolating the present. Life had a predictability to it that was reassuring, even nurturing. The rhythms of the seasons, once determined by the agricultural calendar, shifted to the progression of holidays that framed the year's segments. If we rooted for our local sports teams, they too created a familiarity that was comfortable. We knew the players and could build personalities around them. If this year was disappointing, we could always "wait 'til next year," projecting the progress of the team based on the oncoming prospects.

Now change is a dynamic element, and mere extension of the present often gives us little advice about the future. Even our nexus of holidays has turned on us. Christmas sales begin before Halloween and Washington's Birthday is celebrated on some arbitrarily chosen Monday in February. The future unfolds less as a predictable curve than it does as a bad electrocardiogram, with unpredictable movements and higher peaks and valleys. Change can occur in any direction with any magnitude at any instant. If you think that you can plan your future, you will be surprised constantly. More importantly, you'll be surprised that you're surprised.

Anyone with a nodding interest in sports is aware of the importance of rules and the referees and umpires who enforce those rules. In baseball, some umpires will call the high strike, others will not. In basketball, some referees allow more contact than others do before calling a foul. So the players play three games in one: the game against their own talents, the game against the opponents and the game shaped by the officials. While the games remain the same, the rules shift and the enforcement patterns change, so that the players need to adjust their games every now and again to accommodate the new style.

It is no different with business. The rules change and the tools change. Daniel Burrus, in *Technotrends,* talks about the challenge of combining the new tools of the technological economy with the new rules of business. So it is also with real estate. With the changes that have occurred in the real estate market and the real estate business, the rules with which we conduct our business have changed and the referees are interpreting them in different ways. But what are the new rules, and how do we live with them?

We describe the rules later on. But living with them requires the ability to **manage through change.** If you can achieve the degree of flexibility and fluidity that allows you to adapt to and channel change, then the unexpected will be an opportunity and not a threat. In short, if you position yourself to face a future of change, you will still be surprised at what happens, but you won't be surprised that you're surprised.

The purpose of this book is to help you acquire those skills. It lays out the new rules of the game, the guidelines and questions that will lead you to make decisions about your business that will profit from the opportunities presented by change.

For the most part, this book deals with technologically driven change. Real estate is an information business and nowhere has change impacted on businesses more than in the area of information transferral.

CHANGE IN REAL ESTATE: THE EVOLUTION OF INFORMATION

The rate of change in technology, and thus in the real estate business, has been dizzying and accelerating. Dealing with technological change has never been a significant problem for real estate professionals. Over the years they have absorbed and adapted to a variety of new tools, each of which was a bit more complex than the last. From fax machine to cell phone to digital camera, the REALTOR® has almost seamlessly adopted the latest gadget, has been diligent in learning how to use it and has applied it to become more successful in business.

But now it all seems different. The Internet has provided a whole new avenue for consumers to access property information previously available only through the real estate office. "Outsiders" are taking priority places at the settlement table and in the compensation line. And every day firms are being bought, buying other firms or merging.

Well, it is a whole new world. The reason it seems different now is that the force of technology is changing the entire economy and real estate professionals are caught up in that surge. Since real estate is at its heart an information business, and since technology has most affected the way in which we access and treat information, people in the real estate business have been hit hard by the wave of change. As technology forces the change in business models throughout the economy, it will force changes in the business models used in real estate. It is a time of transition and every part of the business world is involved.

THE SCOPE OF THE NEW ECONOMY

About a dozen years ago, we as a nation began investing more in information processing than in manufacturing. We had ceased to become a manufacturing economy and started to become a knowledge economy. If you want a tangible example of this, look at automobile production. In the old economy, we used large plants, big conveyor belts and massive stockpiles of parts to create cars and trucks. The least important input was the worker. Every eight hours one group replaced another and the line moved on.

Now we do it differently. There are no massive inventories, because the computer at the auto plant talks to the computer at the tire plant and only enough tires are delivered to sustain the day's production. The assembly line has been modified because the car uses several on-board computer chips to control fuel use, temperature, speed, and generally monitor the vehicle's working systems. The assembly process is smarter; the assemblers have to be smart as well and so people are more important. The Saturn plant in Tennessee, where work teams are empowered to speed up, slow down, modify or even stop the line, is a more accurate image of modern auto production.

With this shift to a knowledge economy, geography means less and less. If an industry runs on the brainpower of its human resources, then it can be located anywhere. The industrial cities of the Northeast exist only because they were near the natural resources the economy needed. Now, people are mobile and location can be anywhere. So we get economic centers in Seattle, Silicon Valley, and even outside the borders of the United States. In other words, jobs follow people now, and not vice versa.

Increasingly, those jobs are connected to the manipulation of information and the use of computers. To a great extent, they are involved in the manufacture of computers and peripherals and the creation of software. Sometimes they involve the manufacture of consumer goods, like household appliances, that are themselves dependent on computer chips to perform. In the new economy, the typical consumer works at a job that requires the use of more knowledge than ever before and individually uses pieces of equipment each of which contains more computing power than existed in the entire world prior to 1960. The work model has increasingly become smarter people operating smarter systems.

ROADKILL ON THE INFORMATION HIGHWAY

Dropping out of the work model are the information conveyors–those who were paid to bring information from point A to point B without adding value to it (see Figure 1.1). So we are seeing and will continue to see shrinking numbers of word processors, machine tool assemblers, etc. Add to this list "middlemen"–service providers who have in the past commanded fees by being in a particular position in the information chain. The most obvious case is that of travel agents whose business has been radically reduced by the ease of booking airlines, hotels and rental cars directly

FIGURE 1.1 Changing Technology

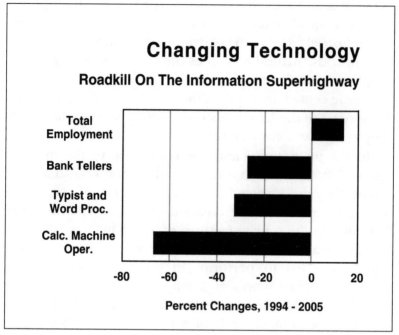

Source: John Tuccillo

through the Internet. And while travel agents will not disappear, their ranks will be depleted as total industry revenues shrink by 30 to 40 percent. Similar statements can be made for stockbrokers, insurance agents, retailers (catalogue sales did these guys in long before the Net) and bankers.

THE OLD REAL ESTATE BUSINESS MODEL

And REALTORS®. The business model under which REALTORS® work is a pre-technology invention. The old model is quite familiar. In fact, you operate under it now. It is a **gateway** model. The consumer contacts the real estate agent or broker and the door to the remainder of the transaction is opened. The real estate practitioner guides the customer through the maze of mortgage application, title search, home inspection and settlement. There is a great deal of handholding, document transportation and arranging involved, but by and large the agent and the broker are amply rewarded for their efforts. That is the case because the real estate practitioner is the gatekeeper and is first on line when compensation is distributed.

The real estate professional stood as the gateway to the real estate transaction: consumers had to contact the agent or broker, and then all the other service providers (mortgage lenders, attorneys, etc.) could be accessed. The REALTOR® controlled the transaction because she controlled the prime resource in the transaction, the property information. To insure that role, the industry translated the information into a foreign language, MLS, meaning that the public had to secure the services of a skilled translator. The compensation the professional received was reward for being the central position in the market. The share of the transaction cost allocated to others was determined by who the real estate professional let in the gateway.

In this old model, the key competencies for real estate success are the ability to listen to and understand people, organizational skills and networking skills. If you were good with people, able to gain their confidence and work closely with them to meet their housing needs, then word of mouth would bring buyers and sellers to your office. If you had wide contacts with mortgage bankers, home inspectors, title companies, etc., then you could ease the transaction to the consumer's satisfaction. And if you were organized enough to keep all the balls in the air, you could be a star. It is instructive that the most popular education courses with real estate agents are those that deal with these skills, particularly time management and organization; the agents know where their profit comes from and they are willing to make the necessary investment to secure their future.

But even if real estate practitioners possessed none of these skills, they still had an advantage in the marketplace. That advantage revolved around property information. As long as the MLS was the single repository of all information about the real estate market, real estate practitioners controlled that source, and the public had to come them. There was no other efficient channel for obtaining information about the possibilities facing consumers in the marketplace, regardless of whether they were interested in the buy side or the sell side. (The consumer could, of course, ride around endlessly looking for signs.) That made the real estate licensee vital to the transaction.

The translation of property information into MLS-speak absolutely locked the information away from the public. The typical listing is all but incomprehensible to the layman. Even if the agent gave the consumer the MLS book to take home and browse through, the book would be nothing more than a paperweight or doorstop. No useful knowledge could be gained from it. As a result, the gateway model was the only viable option in the real estate market.[1]

Technology has broken the information monopoly. The Internet now contains over 100,000 real estate sites, some of which are reviewed regularly by *The Wall Street Journal*. The best of these, REALTOR.COM, contains over a million property descriptions. All are easily accessible by the public, as well as by other settlement service providers. The real estate professional seeking to command payment for listing a home to be sold or screening property for a potential buyer now finds that these services, the heart of the agent's offerings, are being given away.

---

[1] In theory, sale-by-owner (assisted or not) and direct purchase from a builder are market options. But in reality three-quarters of the five million homes bought and sold annually in the United States are transacted with the help of a real estate licensee.

THE AUTOMATION OF REAL ESTATE: A NEW BUSINESS MODEL

Just as the old economy is giving way to the new economy, the old real estate business model is yielding to a new one. The change in the real estate business model that is now being born is simple. The gateway still exists, but it's being supplanted. Now the model looks like a jigsaw puzzle and any number of people have the power to put the puzzle together as the consumer demands. We describe how that is occurring below, and expand on that description in Chapter 2.

Technology will also automate the real estate transaction. Many of the parts of the transaction—mortgage application and approval, title search, appraisal, appointment arranging—can, and will, be more quickly, easily and cheaply done by a clerical worker using the Internet and e-mail than they are now by the physical effort of the real estate licensee. In the future, simultaneous handling of documents and electronic signature recognition will make closing on a piece of property as quick as having a pizza delivered for dinner.

This poses a serious challenge to the real estate practitioner, a challenge felt by bankers, travel agents and stockbrokers. In short, the business model whose value proposition was embedded in the provision of information needs to be changed to a basis of knowledge creation. This means that the typical broker or agent will delegate all the rote functions of the transactions to a machine and the person running it and concentrate instead on creating value for the consumer.

CREATING CUSTOMER VALUE

Increasingly, value for the consumer is identified with reduced time and stress. Customers will pay for a transaction that saves them both time and stress as the result of that transaction thoroughly delights them. The ability to take information off the Internet that will absolutely target the location of all potential buyers for a house will allow the REALTOR® to create a marketing plan that will transcend the mere placement of the property information; effectively playing the counselor to a nervous young couple buying their first home by drawing on all the information streams at your disposal will outweigh a session screening homes on the Net.

NEW MODEL, NEW VALUES

In the new business model the real estate professional is the **transactions manager,** arranging for the details to happen while providing experience, insight and knowledge for the benefit of the customer. The REALTOR®, because of technology, is no longer the gateway to the transaction, but rather must be the one who assembles the jigsaw puzzle that is the home purchase and sale.

Effective use of technology is the key to fulfilling that role. There is information everywhere, very little of it organized. The real estate practitioner can add value to the transaction by accessing that information, arranging it and focusing it on the consumer. There are three categories that can benefit consumers.

1. Clearly, both buyer and seller benefit from effective *marketing*. The use of available information to target prospective buyers for the seller and well-suited houses for the buyer cuts through a great deal of the

FIGURE 1.2   Technology Changes the Transaction

Technology Changes the Transaction
New System

- 🕐 **Marketing Channel**
  - ✳ **Communicate and sell products and services to customers.**

- 🕐 **Distribution Channel**
  - ✳ **Control the flow of goods and services in a supply channel.**

- 🕐 **Communication Channel**
  - ✳ **Coordinate firm's activities and transmit information.**

Common thread is the digital transmission of information.

Source: John Tuccillo

time and anxiety usually connected with the marketing process.

2. Second, clear *communication* reduces the stress felt by the consumer on both sides of the transaction. Setting up links between yourself and your client, and among all settlement service providers, combined with tracking software, will drastically reduce the heartburn and the phone traffic that are tied to the transaction.

3. Finally, providing for the efficient *distribution* of all the materials related to the transaction will speed up the whole process and give real value to the consumer (see Figure 1.2).

The sum of these is the creation of a "back office" operation such as has been a longtime feature of the financial services industries. It requires significant investment, both in technology and in the training related to it. It also requires that the REALTOR® give up some of the things that she has absorbed as part of her professional identity, the face-to-face, people and time–intensive business model. But the recent entrance into real estate of outside capital (Cendant, Insignia, etc.) suggests that the new business model has a real profit potential and appeal.

THE NEW ECONOMIC REVOLUTION

The changes that technology has forced on American business are not trivial. They are reshaping not only how we do things, but also what we actually do. More importantly, they are not transitory. The economy is now changing as fundamentally as it did at the time of the Industrial Revolution. Those that do not adapt will not survive.

Real estate is caught in the vortex of change because of its basic nature as an information industry. But real estate has also been behind the curve of change because of its control of information. Now there is no place to hide. The basic model of the real estate business is changing and will continue to change. Many who resist will fail. But for those who can change, the rewards are great. Think about where you want to be in the future. And remember, participation in the future is not optional.

THE NEW ENVIRONMENT FOR REAL ESTATE

Technology is the main driver of change in our world, but there are other kinds of change that will challenge you. The business model that real estate practitioners have exploited over the years has changed for reasons far beyond technology. The increased interest by players outside the traditional real estate industry has flooded the market with external capital for the first time in memory. This has created a bottom-line pressure that has been heretofore absent, and is forcing all firms to rethink how they operate. While technology has been the tool to remake the business, the essential cause comes from the need to generate a generous return on capital.

Real estate is an information business: changes in the way we treat and exchange information (the most significant impact of technology) have hit at the heart of the business. In a sense, the pressures for change in real estate have been the opposite of the pressures in the general economy. In real estate, we have always valued and relied on people. If the practitioner was good with people, he or she would then only need to be organized and willing to work 60 hours a week to have unlimited earnings potential. Now, moving to a knowledge-based system in the real estate business means adopting more tools and learning new technology.

This change has been dramatic. The Internet pops up and suddenly the old way of presenting property information—the MLS—is under fire; in fact, the charge is led by the industry's own trade association—the National Association of REALTORS®—through its participation in REALTOR.COM, the largest property description site on the Net. E-mail allows mortgage brokers and other settlement service providers direct access to consumers, *your* customers; the center of the transaction no longer *must* be the real estate professional. New vendor companies arise and older companies (Microsoft) diversify into your business, attempting to control the transaction and thus the customer (see Figure 1.3).

FIGURE 1.3 REALTORS® in the Information Age

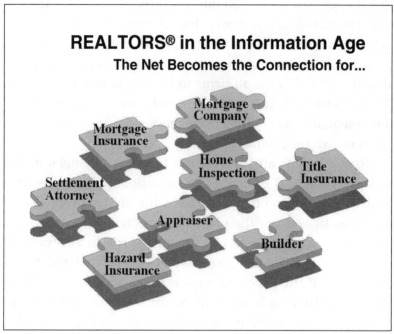

Source: John Tuccillo

THE REAL ESTATE INDUSTRY HAS THE EDGE—EVEN IN THE NEW MODEL

The old model is passing away primarily because all information is increasingly accessible to everyone. The World Wide Web, with its ability to reach everyone everywhere, serves as a vehicle to disseminate property descriptions widely at minimal cost. There is a clear advantage to the consumer to do this: it ensures that anyone looking for a home has the opportunity to encounter his offering, and it allows him to review as wide a variety of options as possible when he is buying.

These advantages are bankable. Both the National Association of REALTORS® (through Real Select, a firm in which it holds a minority interest) and Microsoft perceive that the consumer will use the Web to search for homes to buy and advertise homes for sale. As a result, they are competing directly to populate their own sites with as many properties as possible. Real Select, with its NAR tie, has the market edge and claims well over a million homes, virtually the entire inventory for sale. Microsoft, starting late, is attempting to buy the information from the traditional MLSs. In both cases, having the information means attracting eyes to the site, and thus the ability to sell advertising there.

The entry of Microsoft signals the key change in the new model. Because the information about the real estate market is now widely accessible, the vitality of the real estate practitioner to the transaction because of control over property information is no longer a reality. *Anyone* familiar with either the market or the Web can become an information provider. This has two crucial effects on the industry.

First, it generates significant price pressures. I can now employ the neighbor kid for few hundred dollars to design a page describing in great detail a property I have for sale, adorn it with several flattering pictures, and then place it on a number of high traffic sites on the Web. This means I am less willing to list my house with a licensee for three or four or whatever percent of the selling price. Similarly, if I can review hundreds of properties on the Web, I won't pay a buyer's agent as much. The consumer can do more of the transaction by himself; he will not pay the agent as much because he expects the agent to do less.

The second effect is that democratization of data allows a number of potential transactions managers. There is no longer a single gateway. Countrywide Finance, one of the nation's largest mortgage banking firms, recently conducted an advertising campaign directed at attracting the consumer to apply for a mortgage before looking for a home. This turns the old model on its head. Before, real estate firms offered advice on mortgages to consumers. Now, mortgage bankers can advise consumers on the use of agents. That places the mortgage banker ahead of the real estate practitioner in the line for compensation. It points up the name of the game here: get to the consumer first. If you do so, you will manage the transaction.

The old model was a gateway; the new model is a jigsaw puzzle. Anyone can put the puzzle together. Because technology has allowed for the easy transmission of information (in plain text, not coded MLS-speak), many of the steps of the transaction are easily automated. Searching for information about what houses are for sale can be easily done by using the Internet: virtually the entire inventory is available at no more than two sites. The entire mortgage process—application, analysis of loan options, credit check, approval, disbursement—can be done electronically. If there are questions, video conferencing is available. In the very near future, appraisals and title search will be done online. Somewhat further away, electronic signature recognition and simultaneous document treatment will allow for remote settlement. In other words, the transaction is increasingly independent of the real estate licensee.

THE COMPETENCIES OF THE REAL ESTATE PROFESSIONALS

With the battle to be the transactions manager looming on the near-term horizon, a new set of competencies is needed for the real estate practitioner to hold onto the primary position in the market. It is no longer sufficient to be a conveyor of information in order to command compensation (see Chapter 5). That worked only as long as the public had no easy way to get the information. And while people skills are important, it is crucial to be aware that the people coming into the market may not be the ones you have become accustomed to dealing with. Rather, you need to develop three specific competencies.

1. The first of these is *technological savvy.* This entails knowing what specific machines and techniques will do for your business and incorporating them into your operations. Notice that this does not necessarily mean being computer literate. I would never cut my own hair, yet I know where to get information on styles and instruct my barber (I'm too bald to go to a stylist) on what end result I want. You need to be the same way with technology. Determine the end result you want, understand generally how to get there, and communicate clearly with those who will accomplish it.

2. The second competency is *turning information into knowledge.* There is a difference between the two. Information is a collection of facts or observations about reality. Knowledge is actionable. Gaining knowledge means having the ability to do something positive. Consumers can get all the information they want or need. But it is useless to them unless someone can provide the knowledge to allow them to use it. The manager of the real estate transaction will be the one who can provide that knowledge about the market and the choices available in it. This has always been the strong point for the real estate practitioner. The value added by the agent was not the ability to truck paperwork all over town or to schedule appointments. These are useful, but could be done at a far lower price by a clerk. Rather, **the value of the agent has been in the counseling of buyers and sellers as to price and quality, and the negotiating of the final terms of the deal.** So, you begin with a head start on the new model.

3. The third competency is an *understanding of demographics*. Real estate professionals have always been good people persons. You simply cannot make it in this business without that talent. But the people are changing. The average first-time buyer today is in her early thirties; the average agent is in her late forties. This is a generation gap that can lead to enormous misunderstandings. Younger buyers—in fact, all buyers—are increasingly technologically savvy and will look for their information from electronic sources. You must be at least as sophisticated as the consumer and approach the consumer the way he likes to be approached.

Over the past decade, we have admitted to the United States an average of 600,000 immigrants a year. From what we know about their progress here, it is safe to assume that more and more first-time buyers will be recent immigrants. Most will come from cultures where the customs and beliefs that dictate behavior are far different from yours or from the customers you are used to serving (see Figure 1.4). Without a deep understanding of these cultures, it will be impossible to provide the kind of understanding help that has been the hallmark of the industry.

NEW MODEL, NEW INDUSTRY STRUCTURE

On top of the personnel changes that have been occurring in the real estate industry, its structure has also been changing. Concentration is the order of the day: at present, nearly 70 percent of the membership of the National Association of REALTORS® is located in four percent of the firms (see Figure 1.5). The trend has been growing.

Recent headlines suggest that the trend will accelerate. Cendant, largely through the medium of the National Realty

FIGURE 1.4 Immigrants and Population Growth

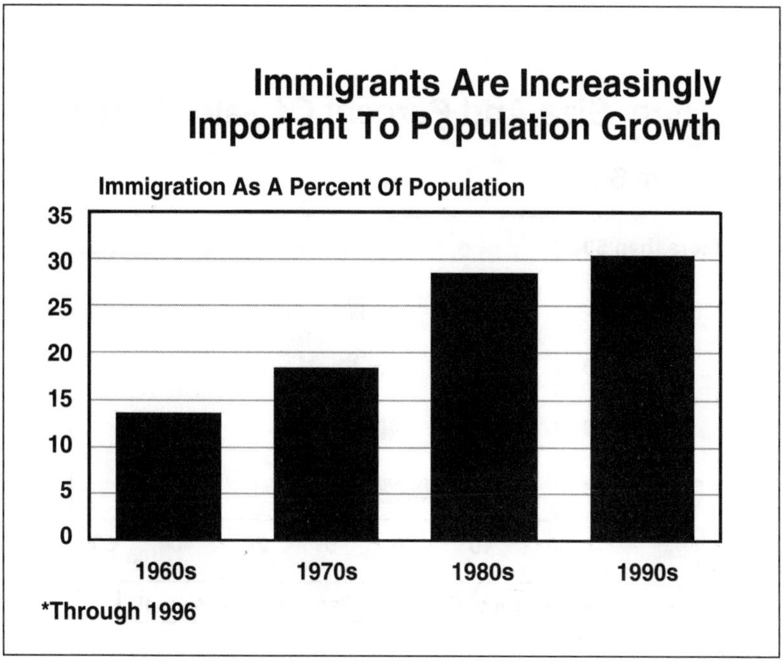

Immigrants Are Increasingly Important To Population Growth

Immigration As A Percent Of Population

(bar chart showing values for 1960s ≈ 13.5, 1970s ≈ 18, 1980s ≈ 28.5, 1990s ≈ 30.5, y-axis from 0 to 35)

*Through 1996

Source: John Tuccillo

Trust (NRT), has been acquiring some significant firms. Most recently, West Shell in Cincinnati and John Grubb in San Francisco have been purchased by the Trust, with Grubb becoming part of C-21 Contempo. O'Connor, Piper and Flynn in Maryland has become an ERA affiliate.

Given that NRT has plenty of cash in reserve and may replenish this stock by going public, this is far from the end. Additionally, Insignia Financial—already a power in real estate management and development—has entered the market with its purchase of Realty One in Cleveland; St. Joe Paper has purchased Prudential Florida through its Arvida subsidiary; and Midstates Power has acquired the holdings of the Amerus Group, which include Iowa Realty and Edina (see Figure 1.6). Al Jolson's immortal first screen sounds,

FIGURE 1.5   Firm Size and Percent of Sales Force

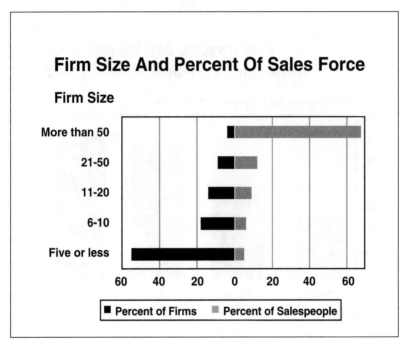

Source: John Tuccillo

"You ain't seen nothin' yet," could probably serve as a good prediction for the real estate business. The structure of the market is increasingly less the mom and pop outfit and more the corporate model.

DRIVERS OF CONSOLIDATION

Why is this all happening now? Three factors are generating the concentration momentum.

Technology

First, *technology* is transforming the real estate transaction. As we described above, the information side of the

FIGURE 1.6   Major Deals in 1997

Major Deals In 1997

Company Name	By	New DBA	Sales Volume
The Prudential John Douglas	NRT	Coldwell - Banker John Douglas	$10.5 b
Cornish & Carey	NRT	Coldwell - Banker Cornish & Carey	$3.3 b
Fox&Lazo/Roach Wheeler BH&G	Merger	Fox & Roach	$2.8 b
Realty One	Insignia	Realty One/Insignia	$2.5 b
Contempo Realty	NRT	Century 21 Contempo	$2.4 b

*NRT = National Realty Trust
Source: Real Trends

Source: Real Trends

business is increasingly automated, and the power the real estate licensee held in the market because of access to the MLS is being diminished. Other settlement service providers, like mortgage originators, can now easily handle major portions of the real estate transaction. Increasingly, real estate is becoming less a face-to-face business and more a one-stop shopping experience in which the consumer has already done part of the work. In the all-purpose office, salaried customer service representatives will handle more functions, leaving the agent free to specialize in the people side of the business.

Capital

Oddly enough, this increase in competition and complexity has attracted *capital* to the industry, the second reason for concentration. As technology standardizes the real estate process, size leads to profitability. Think of the auto industry. Prior to Henry Ford, cars were produced by what was, in effect, a cottage industry. When Ford standardized production, his market and his profits grew. Technology allowed a better business model to emerge and the industry was transformed.

Capital always flows to its most profitable opportunity. It was the promise of a new business model that attracted capital to automobiles and it was capital that made the new model real. Real estate is currently in a similar position, and Cendant and Insignia and others are investing in it for many of the same reasons. Investment in "back office" systems that take some of the more routine parts of the transaction (mortgage application, title search, the arranging of appointments, etc.) and convert them to electronic processing results in increased profitability. It also gives the consumer an experience that he or she can count on every time the real estate firm is used. This arrangement works best with size, market coverage, and (most importantly) capital.

Demographics

The final piece of the puzzle involves industry *demographics*. The real estate industry grew from a cadre of founder-entrepreneurs who accidentally built an industry. Being good at selling properties, they expanded their businesses over time until they were the leaders of large firms with, in some cases, thousands of agents. The entrepreneur-founders of the large firms are aging now and most are reaching the point in life where they want to pull back a bit.

FIGURE 1.7   Factors Generating The Concentration Momentum

Factors Generating The Concentration Momentum

Technology

Technology is transforming the real estate transaction. The information side of the business is increasingly automated; as technology standardizes the real estate process, larger firm size leads to profitability.

Capital

The increase in competition and complexity within the real estate industry has attracted the capital necessary to make the new corporate model work.

Demographics

The real estate industry is aging. Entrepreneur-founders of many larger firms are often looking for an exit strategy, and consolidation occurs with new entrants into the industry, who make appealing offers.

Source: John Tuccillo

They see the business being transformed and aren't sure they have the energy to build again. In many cases, these firms have solid second-level management, sometimes in the form of the founder's children. But in many cases, there is no alternative but to seek out an exit strategy. So the new entrants into the industry, like Cendant and Insignia, find their offers landing on receptive ears. And consolidation occurs (see Figure 1.7).

Demographics combine with technology as well as combining with capital. The real estate business grew in an economy and society where it was a good career for large parts of the population. Women could enter the real estate business, have the flexibility to arrange their time to take care of home and work, and still have excellent earnings potential. Today, the barriers that kept them from the general economy no longer exist and real estate competes for labor with a great many other attractive careers. Since real estate cannot offer fixed hours and guaranteed pay and benefits, it has lost out and the industry is aging. The typical REALTOR® is 49 years old, and that number is rising. The lack of new talent coming into the business makes this a perfect time to automate, and that can be done only with the size necessary to achieve economies of scale and scope.

CONSOLIDATION IS NEITHER GOOD NOR BAD

The criminal investigators in the crowd will recognize that I've established motive, means, and opportunity, and some in the audience will regard this trend toward bigness as a crime. But it's not. Rather, it's a significant shift in the business model. In the 1970s, the U.S. steel and auto industries were overtaken by their German and Japanese counterparts. In the case of steel, we were underpriced. Foreign steel of comparable grade and quality was simply cheaper and customers made business decisions based on this. But in the case of automobiles, it was more than just price. The Japanese introduced a whole new business model, with smaller, lighter, better cars and a new way of distributing them. The entrants into the real estate business are bringing with them an approach and a mindset that will only hasten the adoption of the new business model for real estate.

THE GENERAL RULES

Besides the specific rules that will guide your future in real estate, there are other rules that we all must observe in the technocentric world of business. There are lots of candidates for inclusion here, but first let me offer some general thoughts on how to do business in a technology-dominated world.

First, understand that *your business is global,* whether or not you sell beyond the boundaries of your town. And your business and the world are now ruled by chaos theory. Chaos theory does not refer to the looks of your living room after the holiday presents have been unwrapped by the kids. Chaos theory does not refer to the process you go through to get your client, the buyer, the attorneys and the rest of the cast of characters into a settlement room at the same time. And chaos theory does not refer to the trunk of your car during the spring buying season. Rather, it refers to the way seemingly unrelated events can put into motion major changes—as in world weather patterns affected by the flapping of a butterfly's wings in China.

Case in point. Can you name the currencies of Malaysia, Thailand and Korea? What denominations are they issued in? Whose picture appears on the bills? The odds are few of you passed that little quiz without resort to the encyclopedia. And what's wrong with that? Until recently, these matters were of interest only during exotic vacation trips, if at all. Yet, the fate of these unknown currencies may well determine the degree to which the economic expansion we are enjoying will continue—and whether the state of real estate will be as good as it has been recently.

This all seems a bit silly, doesn't it? How could something so far away be responsible for something so close to home? We live in an integrated global economy; that's not a revelation. But we only realize how true this is when something like the current Asian crisis hits. When speculators began to attack Asian currencies—first Malaysia, then Thailand, then Korea, it panicked stock exchanges all over the globe—first Hong Kong, then Tokyo, then London—until it wound up on our doorstep with the sputtering Dow of the fourth quarter. The chaos sowed in Kuala Lampur cut deeply into the wealth of Toledo, Ohio.

This is important to real estate professionals because the current real estate boom (both residential and, at long last, commercial) is based as much on the increased wealth of consumers as it is on the brightness of the employment picture. Because of pension and 401(k) plans, ownership of stocks has increased from about 20 percent of the population to about 40 percent. So when the Dow began to sky in the Nineties, Main Street felt it as much as Wall Street. With increased wealth, consumers felt freer to spend out of current income, and the economy grew on their backs. Part of this spending is on housing. The existing home sales records set in 1996 and 1997 were, in part, the result of the increased wealth of the consumer coming from the stock market. If that falls, so will spending and growth.

Will that happen? I think the answer is "not to any great degree." The fundamentals—growth, employment, inflation, investment—of all the Southeast Asian economies are sound. Every country in the region has successfully attracted investment from the developed world, has come to grips with its inflation rate and has grown spectacularly. But that was in the early stages of courtship. As the love affair continued, the industrialized suitors began to notice some annoying habits and took a second look. They still liked what they saw, but not as much and not as blindly. In other words, investors began to revalue—and devalue—their opinion of the potential of the economies of Southeast Asia.

This happened once before, two years ago in Mexico. The same process of doubt, devaluation and retrenchment happened. Now the Mexican economy is stronger for it. The excesses of overinvestment were squeezed out and the country has returned to some sort of even keel. The point here is not whether these economies will right themselves. The point is that *we care whether they do because it affects our well being.*

Second, *speed is everything.* Federal Express proved that speed was a competitive advantage as it singlehandedly created a business model based on speed and forced its competitors from United Parcel Service to the United States Postal Service to adopt that model. Now, given the dizzying pace of technological change and improvement, getting to the market first with a new product or system, *even if not completely perfect,* creates a significant market edge.

Netscape made this choice when it flooded the market with its browser (it mailed 40 million to consumers) when the product was only 80 percent complete. It chose speed over completeness because it realized the stakes. The first in the hands of the consumer would set the standard for Internet navigation and capture what has become a multi-trillion dollar market. (It admitted to the incompleteness and enlisted its customers as allies in completing the debugging of the software. More about the value of doing this in Chapter 3.)

It used to be that products could be introduced gradually over time after significant and often painstaking market research was done. Now, that is clearly impossible. The time between the introduction of a product and its evolution to commodity status has shrunk dramatically. In fact, whole business strategies have to be constantly reviewed for applicability. Microsoft, when it realized that the Internet had come to dominate communications technology, abandoned (in a grand public gesture) its proprietary network strategy to embrace a Web-based approach to product development and distribution. In effect, a giant corporation had turned on a dime, not because it wanted to, but because it had to.[2]

---

[2] In *The Digital Economy* (New York: McGraw-Hill, 1996), Daniel Tapscott talks about the three C's of the new economy: computing, communications and content. He points out that there is no longer any value in computing—it's completely a commodity. There is value in communications, however, and this is the realization that led Microsoft to make its U-turn.

Third, *you'll never walk alone*. Business is done, and has been since before GM linked up with Nissan to create the Saturn, through strategic alliances. For most firms, goods and services are produced in conjunction, and increasingly in communication with, other firms. The automobile industry, because of its size and centrality to the United States economy, is the salient example of how this is done. Common computer systems link vehicle manufacturers with parts suppliers, so that shipments respond to the rate of production of the finished product. "Just in time" inventory management is possible because auto manufacturers have joint ventured with their suppliers to create the systems which automatically convey the magnitude and timing of their material needs.

Personal computer standards have also been developed in this manner. Ostensible competitors like Microsoft and Netscape (the current unpleasantness with the Justice Department aside) and Sun Microsystems have all agreed on how the machines should operate. This has dramatically expanded the market, so that each can compete with the others for its share of a larger pie. There are very few cases where businesses today can operate to maximum success in isolation from strategic partners and networks.

Finally, and this is the converse of the second general rule, *abandon your successes quickly*. In 1984, more than half of all recorded sound was contained on vinyl discs. If you were the most efficient manufacturer of vinyl discs then, and your vision was to become the perfect manufacturer of vinyl discs, and you succeeded, you would be out of business today. The world changed and the cassette manufacturers had their day in the sun, only to be swamped almost immediately by the CD-makers. Vinyl records now constitute one percent of recorded sound.

In 1985, Bill Gates approached Steve Jobs and John Sculley and offered domestic licensing rights for his new operating system to Apple Computer, provided he retain the rights to offer it on a worldwide basis. Apple balked, because it would mean ceding market share in the short run at a time when it was coming to dominate the market. Now, the Macintosh is a cult item, Apple has been reorganized several times and struggles to succeed, and the Microsoft-Intel strategic partnership (see rule three above) is a near-monopoly (or more if you believe the Justice Department.)

Because of the compressed life cycle of most products and services in the cyber world, by the time an enterprise is successful, it has lost all profit potential and becomes a barrier to innovation and further success. In short, the cash cows have all gone out to pasture. Yet this is the hardest rule of all to follow. In this world of change and challenge, it is comforting to have a franchise, a product or service niche that offers a sure and sizeable cash flow. And that is the trap. We learn nothing from our successes and we can't give them up. But that is precisely what the new environment is calling for us to do. The best image of this is expressed as follows:

> The harsh news is that getting stuck is a *certainty* in the new economy . . . There is only one way out. The organism must devolve. In order to go from one high peak to another, it must go downhill first and cross a valley before climbing uphill again.[3]

THE EIGHT NEW RULES OF THE REAL ESTATE BUSINESS

For the real estate business, these rules play out in some distinct ways. Since real estate is primarily an information business, it has been hit hard by changing technology. It has been most affected by the declining value of information

---

[3] Kevin Kelly, "New Rules for the New Economy," *Wired*, September 1997, p. 192.

conveyance and most challenged by the need to create value by providing knowledge (actionable bundles of information) to consumers. Many of the new rules stem from this change. These rules are meant to be guides to how you can shape your business to seize upon the opportunities presented by change and thrive in the new environment. Each will be the subject of a chapter in this book; for now, we introduce them so that they can be accessed quickly and understandably.

Rule #1: The Most Powerful Economic Unit Is the Individual (Wadda Ya Mean We, Kemo Sabe?)

Technology has extended the reach of the individual exponentially. On the customer side, pull technologies have allowed consumers to dictate to manufacturers and retailers the what, when, where and how of sales. Catalogue sales increased in the first four years of the 1990s from $12 billion to over $60 billion, and televised shopping services are beginning to truly sting retailers. Why? Because they give individuals control over their own activities. University professors now can download (and simultaneously get copyright permission) from the Internet just those articles they need for their classes and reprint them for their students, thus bypassing the arbitrary, homogenous decisions of book publishers. Electronic commerce, once a dream, now provides a significant portion of Web traffic and is growing rapidly, with software, recorded sound, travel and books leading the hit parade. By 2005, e-commerce will exceed $300 billion.

On the producer side, desktop publishing has allowed individuals to produce the opinion and analysis they want with the look they have in mind, and has liberated them from the concepts of graphic designers (not always with improved results). Perhaps the most compelling example of this is *virtualvint,* a Web site representing a group of micro wineries in California. The vintners can now directly reach the public without being required to generate minimum production levels in order to be marketed by a wholesaler.

For the real estate industry, this presents a real challenge. Under current business models, all information flows through some intermediary in the marketplace: real estate professional, mortgage banker, relocation firm, etc. Now, much of the information and analysis of the real estate market can be done by the individual prior to any contact. This will inevitably alter compensation patterns and thus the way in which the business is organized. The lesson here is that you need to recognize the enhanced economic power of the individual and accommodate it within your business model.

Rule #2: Lock the Customer In For Life By Creating Unique Value

Recently, *The Wall Street Journal* reported that Harrah's was building a database on its customers that would allow it to chart all their tastes and thus be able to create a perfect experience for them every time they visited the hotel or casino. This data base would include not only food and room preferences, but also gaming results and any comments passed on by the guest in the course of a visit. Moreover, other databases containing demographic and economic data would be linked to Harrah's so that as complete a picture as possible might be drawn of the guest.

Publix, a supermarket chain in Florida, has long done a similar compilation based on groceries purchased linked with information on residence and income. This enables Publix to target its customers tightly when sending coupons or free samples. Lands' End, L. L. Bean and other catalogue marketers use similar systems in order to establish a customer familiarity that creates and sustains brand loyalty. But can't that customer be drawn away by a competitor with a similar system? Yes, but since the customer has gone to some effort to provide data to the company, duplicating this data means sustaining the same costs. In other words, successful one-to-one marketing creates a competitive edge and sets up a barrier to competition.

When Netscape released its Navigator software, it did so before the program was perfected. Rather, it saw the need to beat everyone else to the market if they were to become the standard for Internet browsing. So it mailed out 40 million copies of something about 80 percent complete. It also invited its customers to suggest improvement: in effect, partnering with them to create the final product. Whenever an improvement appeared in a later version of the browser, some customers out there saw their ideas in practice. This bound the customer more closely to the company and the product.

Real estate suffers from the fact that sales are made infrequently, so the buildup of customer loyalty cannot be helped by often-repeated contacts. But in most cases, real estate business is done by referral—through friends, family or other firms. Those referrals can come more frequently if the real estate firm is able to customize each transaction so that it can only have taken place for that one particular individual.

Rule #3: The Middle is Disappearing

As you might have guessed, technology has reamed out the intermediary agent in the transaction. The recession of 1990 began in the Northeast and it began in the financial services sector. Technology exposed a whole stratum of executives (usually with the title of vice president) as information conveyors—in effect, white-collar burger flippers—in a world where that function didn't pay any more.

So it is in a variety of other areas. When you can buy insurance and book plane tickets and hotels on the Web, what's the need for insurance salesmen and travel agents? While more exotic transactions require the need of a professional, a large percentage of deals disappear, and with them industry revenues. And it goes further. In the election of 1994, when the Republicans captured control of the Congress, the Democrats they defeated were largely moderates–party extremists were handily reelected. Not only was the party makeup of the Congress changed, so too was the ideological climate. In the job market, we see an increasing dichotomy between relatively high-paid technically savvy jobs and low-paid semiskilled service occupations.

As the middle vanishes from so much of American life, it also disappears from the real estate industry. In brokerage firms, mortgage originators, relocation companies and many other real estate service providers, the economies of scale related to information are driving the market into very large, all-purpose, market share firms and smaller, highly specialized, boutique-type firms. There is nothing on the horizon that will alter that trend.

Rule #4: Think Content

The three elements of information technology are computing, communication and content. The first of these–computing–concerns software development. The Internet has killed this business and made software a public good: you go online and get any program you want free (see Rule one in the intro). Microsoft's shift in focus two years ago was recognition of this. The second element–communications–concerns the race to set standards for networks. Netscape's gamble was an attempt to exploit the profitability of this business, as is Microsoft's entire strategy. There are a large number of competitors in this field, so many that it resembles the automobile industry at the turn of the Twentieth Century. We just have not yet discovered our Henry Ford.

The last area–content–is where the real value added lies. Without content, even the best network in the world is nothing more than a telephone system—dumb wires and poles. Real estate firms can position themselves as content providers and thus be important players in the new economy. Essentially, they need to create knowledge by taking information and molding it into value for consumers.

Rule #5: Mine Your Bits

One of the major changes in the economy has been the shift from atoms to bits.[4] Think of information in a book as atoms—it has mass, shape, texture, etc. Now consider information on the World Wide Web—these are bits, electronic impulses that have no tangible existence. More than matter separates these two. A book is static; information is there. But bits can be combined and recombined into an ever-changing array of knowledge, used in different ways at different times.

Hate those annoying telemarketing calls at dinnertime? Ever wonder how they got your name? The answer is simple: someone, somewhere got the information, assembled it into databases and sold it to the marketing company. You can do this with bits. And to the extent that business can be generated through these appeals (not from me, but maybe it could!) these bits have value.

Historically, REALTORS® have gathered tons of data. The MLS systems record sales statistics, including property and buyer and seller information. More detailed descriptions of households, including income, home values, etc., exist in the files of the real estate office. These are bits. All this information is valuable both as a product itself and as a device to bind the client closer to you.

---

[4] The prime statement of this shift and its implications is found in Nicholas Negroponte, *Being Digital* (New York: Alfred A. Knopf, 1995).

Rule #6: Sell the Experience, Not the Product

When you go to a Disney theme park, you don't get rides that are appreciably different from those at Coney Island in New York, King's Island in Cleveland, or any of dozens of other parks throughout the United States. Rather, you enter (their words, not mine) a "Magic Kingdom." You get an experience. From the time you enter the grounds and park your car in the Goofy lot, to the time you drive out, you have purchased an *experience*. There are no employees. Rather, there are "cast members," from the guy in the Mickey suit to the maid who makes up your hotel room.

In the new economy, product has melded with delivery system to create experience. Starbucks is as much ambiance as coffee (or that linguistic abomination, "espresso drink"); Nordstrom is the personal shopper and the piano player, and also clothing. The parts are inseparable.

The real estate business is slowly learning this lesson. There are no real estate firms in this country where consumers receive the same experience (in the sense of Disney or Starbucks or Nordstrom) each time they enter. No two offices produce the same experience; no single office can promise the same experience each time. Yet, in a world of change and chaos, brands that offer a steady and reliable experience are sought out and used by consumers.

Rule #7: Feed the OODA Loop

"Observe, orient, decide and act." In a world where microscopic edges often yield big profits and then disappear rapidly (see the last general rule above), the ability to recognize those edges and act on them is an enormous competency. It is also an essential one. The best example of this is Verifone, the company that makes the software to validate your credit card when you present it for payment. Its culture is urgency, teamwork and market sense. Half of the staff is on the road 80 percent of the time, working closely with customers to understand their needs and to solve their problems before they even know the problems exist. To increase the speed of response, all company information is available to all employees, and e-mail flows freely through all levels of the organization.

Real estate has never been, in its mainstream, an innovative business. Only when something is tried and proven successful will the industry adopt and adapt. This happened 25 years ago with Re/Max, and the industry is still recovering, having followed the innovation in the wrong way. Re/Max is a system designed to free top–producing agents from traditional broker control. This system was interpreted as allowing good agents higher commission splits. By interpreting Re/Max's success as a *relative* phenomenon, not an *absolute* phenomenon (as it was), traditional brokers rewarded good, but not great, agents and cut deeply into their own profits. The paradox here is that those who do feed the OODA loop are the most successful. They are the top-producing agents and the most successful firms.

Rule #8: Know What Business You're In

This is an evergreen rule that takes on added significance in a technocentric world. We don't fly on Union Pacific Airlines. The reason is that at the turn of the Twentieth Century, Union Pacific defined its business as railroads. So, a few years later it took no notice of the experiments taking place on the North Carolina coast. If it had been in the business of transporting people and things (which of course it was) then it could possibly have incorporated the Wright Brothers into its business development division.

There are more modern examples as well. American Express, by defining itself in the document delivery and financial services businesses, was able to stay focused on its business yet change its entire delivery system. McDonald's took food service technology and franchised it, reinventing themselves as a real estate company, owning ground leases and using advertising to drive people through their real estate.

We've said before that real estate is an information business, and it is. But information is now automated, removing the rewards for simply possessing information. So where's the core business? The answer is *knowledge,* the creation of packages of information (bits, not atoms) that are of value to consumers because they are actionable. Regardless of what happens to the business model of the real estate industry or the degree to which portions of the transactions are automated, the wisdom and counsel of someone or some firm with expertise in the real estate market will provide that value added. The challenge is to make that transition.

CAN'T I SURVIVE WITHOUT ALL THIS TROUBLE?

Right about now, you're saying to yourself: Do I have to? I've managed to create a nice business by doing what everyone else has done. Why can't I just go on being me, doing what I know and ride off into the sunset? The answer, of course, is yes, yes you can. No less an authority than the Bible confirms this:

> What was, will be again,
>
> What has been done, will be done again,
>
> And there is nothing new under the sun!
>
> Take anything which people acclaim as being new:
>
> it existed in the centuries preceding us
>
> —Ecclesiastes, 1: 9-10

So you don't have to think about a thing in this book. But before you do that, consider how the real estate business developed. We like to call it a mom-and-pop industry and in one way that's true. More than 60 percent of the 90,000 or so real estate companies in this country have fewer than five salespeople associated with them. Even the largest firms trace their roots back to a founder–entrepreneur who started in the business with no capital, but with a knack for brokering real estate. Eventually, as he became real good and real busy, he opened up more offices and took on more associates. But no matter how large he became, he was still the owner of a small business.

Even in the cases where the firm took on the look of a large regional, the operation still had more in common with the local supermarket than it did Sam's Club. When franchises came along, national companies were created, but they still were aggregations of moms and pops. The national advertising was in place, the services benefited from economies of scale, and there was a national convention. Still, the model had not changed.

So much for the past. As we go forward, the forces of change will inexorably push the real estate business into the swirl and chaos that marks the new economy. There is pressure to attract young talent into the business. No problem. Let's set up benefit plans. But that means some regularity of earnings. To get there, let's try salaried employees. That makes sense if we can automate the transaction. If we automate the transaction, we can brand a product. Branding will give us a leg up in the market. Then everyone will brand.

All these changes—benefit plans, salaried employees, automated transactions, branding of real estate, as well as telecommuting, national expansion, strategic alliances—are being experimented with out there. This happens because the economy forces it and technology enables it.

When we write the history of the real estate industry during the next ten years, it won't be a history of moms and pops. Rather it will be the story of how a business that had grown gradually on the backs of small entrepreneurs suddenly turned about to become a modern corporate industry. These rules will help you through that turnaround. Ignore them at your own risk.

HOW DO I USE THIS BOOK?

The rules can stand independently, but are best thought of in tandem. Thus, when you understand the power of one (Chapter 2), you can plan to lock in the customer for life (Chapter 3) by mining your bits (Chapter 6). Similarly, knowing what business you're in (Chapter 9) will allow you to sell the experience, not the product (Chapter 7). At the end of each chapter, we suggest the most closely related of the other rules.

The key is to consider the implications of each of the rules for your own special case. Brokers will perhaps find more here than will agents, in part because economies of scale place them in a better position to leverage technology. But agents will benefit as well from understanding the changing model of the business and how the new rules can help them lock their customers in for life. Ask yourself the following questions for each of the rules:

- What does this rule mean for my business?
- Are the examples given relevant to my particular situation?
- How can I best act on the rule to profit from it?
- How fast do I need to act?
- With whom do I need to cooperate or partner in order to best exploit this rule?

Answering these questions will lead you to the best solutions to the new environment. Good luck!

The Most Powerful Economic Unit Is the Individual (or Wadda Ya Mean We, Kemo Sabe?)

> . . . because technologies get smaller, faster and cheaper technological innovation augments our ability to do things for ourselves. The result is that we are less dependent on professionals and institutions.[1]
>
> —Michael H. Annison, *Managing the Whirlwind*

BROADCAST NEWS

The real estate business is not the only one that grew up with a "gateway" model. And, not coincidentally, there are changes going on in other areas as well. Again, like real estate, the shift is moving the industry from the gateway to the transactions management model.

One of the most familiar of American institutions is the television network. Most Americans grew up in the thrall of "the tube," with TV serving as an electronic babysitter for latchkey kids of several generations. Much of our society and culture revolves around broadcast images, and TV references pepper our speech: witness the hoopla surrounding the last episodes of *M*A*S*H, Dallas* and *Seinfeld;* billions around the world watch the Super Bowl. Yet, despite this importance in our culture, we often overlook a simple fact: the business model upon which the major networks are built is failing.

---

[1] Reprinted with permission from the Medical Group Management Association, 104 Inverness Terrace East, Englewood, Colorado 80112-5306; 303-799-1111. Copyright 1993.

Consider how NBC, CBS and ABC built their television networks (all were, of course, radio networks first). They controlled a distribution system through which they could pump images and sound that would interest people. The technology they controlled enabled them to reach into virtually every American household. Since these households consisted of consumers, companies who wished to sell products would buy time on the distribution system. It was a very simple business model.

Over time, that model eroded. First, television set manufacturers implemented the remote control, and viewers could switch away from advertising. The networks countered this by counterprogramming ads. Even now, at eight and twenty-two minutes after the hour, ads are running on all three networks. Next came the VCR, enabling households to tape programs and view them later, speeding through the advertising and nonessential segments (which could reduce many shows down to about a minute in actual viewing time). Both of these innovations made the network structure less attractive to advertisers.

But the real blitz was yet to come. Cable television expanded the choices available to the consumer. The major networks became only three among many. Specialty channels have abounded and one can watch, golf, business, jurisprudence, comedy, sports, cooking and, of course, movies, exclusively on a given channel. In fact, it is theoretically possible that viewers can design their own channel with whatever looks good.

Add to that satellite dishes, which expand the options beyond the United States, and the networks are further submerged into the din. The value of appearing on the old-line networks has diminished further. Ratings are down, and advertising rates have fallen. It's instructive that two of the three traditional networks (ABC to Disney and NBC to GE) are now controlled by corporations who themselves have significant stakes in cable TV.

*D*oris Kearns Goodwin, in her memoir *Wait 'Til Next Year* (New York: Simon and Schuster, 1997) presents a wonderful description of how television came to her Long Island neighborhood:

> Television had come to the neighborhood.
>
> That night, the parents and children of Southard Avenue crowded into the Goldschmidts' living room, and watched as vaguely defined, snowy figures cavorted across the seven inch black-and-white screen embedded in an odd block of furniture. "A marvel," the adults assured one another . . . But to me and my playmates it was only another wonder in a world of constantly unfolding wonders. . . (p. 120)

Sounds a lot like our reaction to laptops or cell phones or any of a host of other "wonders." I well remember a scene similar to that described above, as do many reading this book.

HOW COULD THIS HAPPEN?

The point of this story is not to generate pity for the networks. Rather, it is an example, perhaps the most familiar example, of how the leverage of the individual consumer has grown over time to the detriment of the producer. In the broadcast case, the viewer was initially at the complete mercy of the network: the choice was either to watch or not watch. And since television was a miracle in the postwar world, people were inclined to watch. Consumers could not—nor did they care to—exert their taste; their tastes were dictated by the decisions of network executives. But soon they were hooked and accepted the business model without hesitation.

But, as new inventions entered the market, the power of the consumer increased. The entire entertainment decision is now in the hands of the consumer. Is it broadcast fare, specialty viewing or even rental movies tonight? Ah, choices are hell! The business model that governs the networks has been irrevocably altered by the shift in power from the sender to the receiver.

*P*ointcast is a service that allows a computer user to create a "headline" crawl that brings news and information continually across the screen when the user is online. For example, I could package price quotes on the stocks I hold, sports scores and up-to-date information on the Japanese economic crisis, to be sent to me in a steady stream or at a regular interval. Real estate professionals might want current mortgage quotes or real estate news services in their mix. This service is a mixture of pull and push technologies. The news is pushed at you, but only because you have pulled it down.

By extension, market leverage has shifted from the producer to the consumer. Technology has extended the reach of the individual exponentially. The difference is what is referred to in computer terminology as *push* and *pull* technology. Push technology represents the old system: the customer consumes whatever is pushed at him. Pull technology is the other side of the coin: the customer decides what she wants to receive and pulls it down. The Internet is the most prominent example of this. We go on the Web and we decide what it is we want to see, what information we wish to receive, who we wish to contact. Even the new "push" technologies, like Pointcast, are really customer-dictated in that the receiver controls the content.

As we'll see later in this chapter, there is a direct analogy to real estate here. The networks were undone by competition from outside their ranks and they now operate in a market populated by a variety of competitors. The real estate industry is now, because of information technology, up against a variety of nontraditional competitors for its core business. All of these competitors have recognized the power of one and are exploiting it. Real estate needs to respond.

THE POWER OF ONE CONSUMER

The net of all this (no pun intended) is that market power now resides in the individual rather than in the corporation. Pull technologies have expanded the options open to the consumer for receiving information, arranging time and determining value. This has allowed consumers to dictate to manufacturers and retailers the what, when, where and how of sales.

It occurs in ways as small as the distribution of consumers' time. Traditionally, shopping was confined to the hours a store chose to remain open and customers were able to bank in an even narrower time frame. During the Seventies and Eighties, this became a problem when two-earner households became the norm. Responding to household needs, store owners tried expanded hours, Sunday openings and even 24-hour supermarkets. The widespread use of the ATM meant banking could be done around the clock.

The real convenience for consumers has been catalogue sales. They increased in the first four years of the Nineties from $12 billion to over $60 billion, and televised shopping services have become a regular feature of the marketing mix. Why? They give shoppers individual control over their activities. With catalogues and TV, consumers can shop when and where they want. I am a perfect example of that. Because I travel extensively, I do all my shopping on airplanes. Armed with catalogues, I can use the privacy of the plane trip to decide on goods I want and then phone a series of toll-free numbers and have the goods delivered to my door. And because catalogue sales are mechanized, even more attention is paid to me. When I call a place for the second time, the odds are that my purchase history prompts the operator to deal with me as an old friend (see Chapter 3, "Lock the Customer in for Life").

The result has been to place pressure on retail establishments, but only some. Catalogues cannot offer the human presence, so smaller establishments that allow the consumer to connect with the sales staff are still very attractive. Establishments like Wal-Mart that offer high value are also prized by consumers. It is the all-purpose department store that loses in the new world, and we have seen chain after chain go out of business. In other words, the middle is disappearing (see Chapter 4).

ELECTRONIC COMMERCE IS THE REAL DEAL

The next development is even more significant and is happening now: electronic commerce. Electronic commerce is defined as the use of telecommunications, extranets and private networks to effect transactions. Once a dream, e-commerce (as it's called) now provides a significant portion of Web traffic and is growing rapidly, with software, recorded sound, travel and books leading the hit parade. Amazon.com has created a whole new way of shopping for books. Consumers can log onto a Web site and order any book in print, with delivery within three days. If you don't know what you want, you can search by topic, author or partial title. As the consumer uses the service more, Amazon develops a profile and recommends books for purchase at the next contact. (For the importance of this, see Chapter 3.) This process has been so successful that Amazon has branched out into music. Traditional booksellers like Barnes and Noble have had to respond with similar Web-based "stores."

*I*ra Magaziner, President Clinton's principal advisor on the Internet, predicts that by the year 2000 there will be 1 billion people around the world with access to the Internet, leading inevitably to tremendous growth in commercial activity. He identifies four categories of electronic commerce:

> The actual delivery of services across the Internet, allowing consumers to download software, movies or music services, medical diagnostic services, educational services and financial services;
> Business-to-business transactions;
> Individual consumer purchases of physical goods via the Internet, in many cases a substitute for retailing;
> Businesses that grow up around discrete communities of interest.

(Summary courtesy of Eric Marcus, Advantec Strategies Corp., Lake Forest, IL.)

The ability of Web sites like Car Point to move consumers from auto lots to their computers to buy cars has already changed the behavior of car dealers. The Rosenthal organization in the Washington metropolitan area consists of ten dealerships. It has recently added an eleventh, with a total staff of four. The last operation is the Web site and the four employees handle all the deals generated from the site. By early next century, e-commerce will amount to over $300 billion. As it grows, it will further increase the power individuals have to dictate the terms of sale of consumer goods.

Consumption goods are only one aspect of the economic power of the individual. University professors were traditionally subject to the choices made by textbook editors. Usually those choices are designed to generate as large a market as possible and the books look like grab bags containing something for everyone. As a result, the individual teacher would be forced either to assign a book and use only portions of it, or alter the curriculum to suit the text.

Now, professors can download from the Internet just those articles they need for their classes and reprint them for their students, thus bypassing the arbitrary, homogenous decisions of book publishers. The ability of faculty members to adjust their presentation material on a continuous basis allows them to improve the timeliness and quality of higher education. Like the TV viewer designing his own channel, the professor can now "write" a text specifically designed for every course he teaches.

THE POWER OF ONE PRODUCER

Remember the story of the Wizard of Oz? The meek medicine man from Nebraska (yes, he was from Nebraska—he only met Dorothy in Kansas) projects an image of great power and majesty despite being a mere mortal. The residents of the Emerald City respect and fear the power of the Wizard. When Toto tugs open the curtain, the Wizard is revealed for the snake oil salesman he really is, but until then all thought him to be the great and powerful Oz. He said so, and no one wanted to mess with someone so authoritative.

So it is today. Pull technology can do for the small business what it has done for the consumer. Desktop publishing, the ease of developing a Web site and the anonymity of the Internet have all allowed individuals to project that same image as the Wizard of Oz. They can produce and distribute the opinion and analysis they want with the "look" they have in mind, and this has liberated them from the concepts of graphic designers. But revolutions have been started with less.

Most of these newsletters and "zines" (the new term for electronic magazines with a single interest focus) are aimed at the hobbyist, defined in the broadest sense (e.g., Leonardo DiCaprio zealots). But the power of one can also have societal consequences. We have seen the results of the power of the individual to create a national dialogue. The O. J. Simpson trial, the death of Princess Diana and the recent accusations against the Clinton administration have all spawned a cottage industry of analysis, rumor, innuendo and conspiracy theory. The new pundits have formed opinion and in some cases have even created the news themselves.

Small manufacturers especially have benefited from technology. They now have easier and cheaper access to their potential markets. Perhaps the most compelling example of this is *virtual vint.com*. This is the Web site of a group of micro wineries in California. Previously they could reach buyers for their wines only through wholesalers who dictated the terms under which they could reach their market. This was costly and, in some cases, not even possible. As a response, the vintners joined together to create

FIGURE 2.1   Traditional Transaction

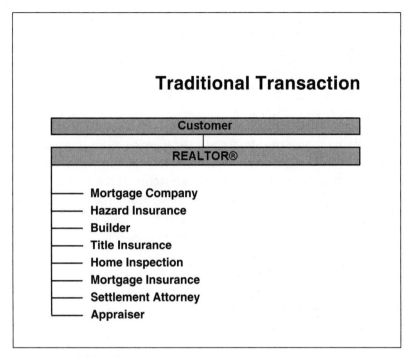

Source: John Tuccillo

and advertise their own Web site. The site can now directly reach the public and allow them to order directly from the individual vintners. In addition, vintners are no longer required to generate minimum production levels in order to be marketed by a wholesaler.

THE DEATH OF THE REAL ESTATE BUSINESS MODEL

The broadcast industry is not alone in seeing its business model disintegrate. This is precisely what is happening in real estate, and its origin is in the power of one. In the real estate market even today, the real estate practitioner stands as the gatekeeper to the transaction. The customer—buyer or seller—comes to the agent or the broker who then opens the entire transaction up. The gateway opens and behind it are all the settlement service providers the consumer needs to achieve her ends. Mortgage bankers, appraisers, title insurers, attorneys and others are lined up at the direction of the real estate professional (see Figure 2.1).

Without this gatekeeper function, it is very difficult for the consumer to complete the purchase or sale. It would be possible to do it through other providers, but not nearly as efficient as using the real estate company. (Historically, only about one out of six houses is sold without the benefit of a licensee.) And, of course, the compensation flowing from the transaction goes primarily to the gatekeeper.

*R*ecently, Countrywide Financing, one of the country's largest mortgage bankers, implemented an advertising campaign urging the consumer to qualify for a loan before finding a house. This is a clear attempt to position the lender as the transaction manager, but has not been successful, largely because it lacked a support system. It also points up the power of one in that it was worth the expenditure to become the first point of contact for the homebuyer. • • • • •

The reason for the real estate professional assuming this role is the control of information. The consumer *must* come to the real estate office to find out what's available on the market or to advertise his own sales offering. The real estate professional enjoys "position power." Because she controls the information, she could command compen-

FIGURE 2.2   Technology Changes the Transaction (Old System)

Technology Changes the Transaction

Old System

LONG + FOSTER

```
-------------------------------------------------------------------
     LISTING REPORT FOR ML# :N689627 - JUN 1, 1996 - 3:48 PM - PAGE 1
-------------------------------------------------------------------

LONG & FOSTER REAL ESTATE, INC  703-522-0500                  RD: 01 JUN 96
# N689627   L&F 08   ER   2707 BRYAN PL           3-3    $235,000    A /SFDT
PA: ALEXANDRIA                     CY: ALEXANDRIA       VA        ZP: 22302
LG: HXL713         PS: A V BRYAN              TAX.ID#: AL17264500
MC: 24D3           AG: 42        YR.BLT: 1954  NEW.CONST: N       OS: NOT CONDO
AC: 0.1837         LS: 8,006        TM: 52.00-4-29          DES.REP: Y
ES: MACARTHU       MS: WASHINGT       HS: WILLIAMS    SELL: 3%      BUY: 3%
HD:                MN: SPACIOUS       NL: 2            LR: 20X12/MN  DR: 11X10/MN
1B: 13X11/MN  1B.SIT:                 2B: 12X12/MN     3B: 11X9/MN   4B:
KT: 10X9/MN        RR: 23X21/L1       FR: 16X14/MN     DN: 15X8/L1   5B:
BR: 3              FBA: 2        BR.MAIN: 3       BR.UP: 0      BR.LOW: 0
BA:                HBA: 1        BA.MAIN: 2       BA.UP: 0      BA.LOW: .5
BASE: Y        #CRPT: 0  #GAR: 0   GAR:               #FPL: 1          TT: $2,685.70
POA: N             FE: $0       OTH.FEE: 0       TOT.FEE: 0          TY: 1996
1T: $0             PI: $             IR:              OD:
2T: $              OT: 0             CA: $235,000     EQ: $235,000
LA: BETSY TWIGG            284-9389         PGR:816-6254      BP:212-8956
ON: OWNERS             PH: 549-9517     LO: BRUCE A AND MARCIA G BROWN
ORIG.LP: $235,000     PRIOR.LP: $             ED: 01 JUN 96
```

Source: John Tuccillo

sation—substantial compensation. In fact, the real estate profession ensured that power by translating property information into a foreign language. The MLS, with its abbreviations and shorthand, is virtually incomprehensible to the layman (see Figure 2.2.) On the other hand, every real estate practitioner is at least bilingual, speaking English and MLS-speak.

So, as long as the MLS was the only source of property information, the REALTOR® remained the gateway to the transaction. To get to the other providers of settlement services, the consumer had to go through the REALTOR®'s door. In part, that's why agency developed as it did in real estate law. Traditionally, every real estate agent represents the interest of the seller, or is a subagent of the seller. There was

I would argue that the increased leverage of the buyer in the market because of technology has fostered the growth of buyer's agency. When the game is one-sided, there's no sense joining the losing side. When things even up, you can profit from serving either side. It is no accident that the rise of buyer's agency tracks with the increased accessibility to property information by buyers.

no buyer representation, because all the information was connected with the seller and the home that was on the market.

THE BUYER DOES MORE

Now consider how the power of one changes the rules of the transaction. Homebuyers and sellers are the consumers of the real estate market and they have been the objects of information and processes "pushed" at them by real estate practitioners and the other settlement service providers. Just as the Internet has allowed the consumer options for the purchase of consumer goods, it offers them options for the acquisition of real estate services.

Start with the search process for the potential buyer. There is a variety—seemingly limitless—of Web sites that display property information. In fact, REALTOR.COM, the site maintained by Real Select, a company partially owned by the National Association of REALTORS®, contains virtually the entire inventory of existing homes for sale. While others are more specialized, the sum of them all gives the individual the power to conduct her own search process. (Microsoft

FIGURE 2.3 Technology Changes the Transaction (New System)

Technology Changes the Transaction
New System

$269,900 Located in **POLO FIELDS, RESTON**, County: **FAIRFAX**, Zip Code: **20191**.

This three story detached, colonial home built in 1995 has 4 bedroom(s), 2 full bath(s), 1 half bath(s) and is approximately 2840 sq. ft.

This home has a basement. Rooms include a family room, formal dining room, breakfast area, den/study/library, office, master bedroom suite, master bathroom, laundry room.Other features include 1 fireplace(s), 9'+ ceilings, window treatments. This home has a 2 car garage. Recreation amenities include community swimming pool(s), community indoor swimming pool, community tennis court(s), community golf, community children's play area, community clubhouse(s), biking/fitness trail, access to riding trail. The lot is professionally landscaped. The property is located on 0.3 acre(s), planned development community.MLS#:FX2160188

Source: John Tuccillo

has not yet gotten up to speed as a competitor in this market.)

The consumer can go to the site, search by price and location (See Figure 2.3), and then show up at the real estate office with his search already narrowed to a very few homes. Soon, all the sites available to the consumer will have multiple pictures of the home, video tours and even virtual reality tours. The screening process, long a service of the real estate practitioner who possessed the information about the market, is now done by the customer and no longer commands compensation in the marketplace.

Additionally, there are numerous mortgage company Web sites that allow individuals to apply for financing from the privacy of their home. The linkage of mortgage lenders with credit bureaus allows for the qualification process to take place quickly and seamlessly. Soon, there will be automated appraisal and title verification sites that will give individuals the power to do those functions on their own.

AND SO DOES THE SELLER

Now consider the selling side of the transaction. Again traditionally, the real estate agent prepares a listing presentation designed to show how the home will be entered into the MLS and marketed. Now the homeowner can access a number of technical service providers who will design a Web page advertising the home, with full motion video, and link that Web page to any number of often visited real estate Web sites, with a hot wired key to provide e-mail back to the owner. In fact, the homeowner can get little Jimmy next door to design a Web page describing the house you want to sell and hack it everywhere on the Internet (up to and including the central computer at the Pentagon) for $100— it's not that big a deal to little Jimmy. The potential listing agent now must respond to that type of competition.

The shift from push to pull and the application of the power of one in the real estate market put strong pressure on the compensation received by real estate professionals. The existence of little Jimmy means that listing fees will have to be competitive. The ability of the consumer to search the Net for houses means that the agent may be called on to do less, with the consumer less willing to pay.

Most importantly, the expansion of information access has changed the business model under which the real estate profession works. The real estate process is not a gateway anymore. Rather, it's a jigsaw puzzle with a random group of pieces (see Figure 2.4). Anyone acquainted with the real estate market has the capacity to manage the transaction and put the puzzle together to the consumer's benefit. The

FIGURE 2.4 REALTORS® in the Information Age

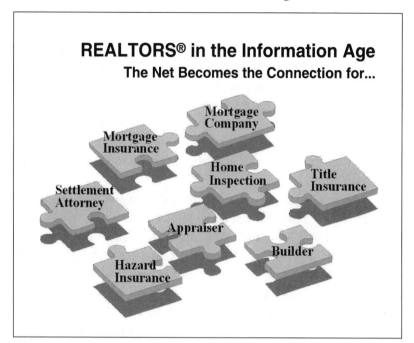

Source: John Tuccillo

ability of other service providers—mortgage bankers, attorneys, title companies, etc.—to manage the transactions shakes up the distribution of payments related to the real estate transaction. It potentially puts the real estate professional farther back in line when the payout occurs.

REAL ESTATE PROFESSIONALS ALSO HAVE THE POWER OF ONE

Fortunately, the power of one works for the real estate practitioner as well. Technology has not only changed the way we communicate, it has changed the products we use. This gives producers of goods and services the ability to respond as technology raises the bar of customer expectations. Specifically, the products and services we produce are higher in information content. That ranges from the machine that wakens you with fresh-brewed coffee at a certain time to the computer in your car that tells you where you are and how to get where you're going. There are six times the number of computer chips in the world as there are computers. The excess chips wind up in the oddest places, including your hotel room, which has more computing power than the standard industrial computer of 1970.

Consumers increasingly expect that what they buy will be "smarter." For real estate professionals, it is no longer enough to have MLS information and to haul papers from the customer to the attorney to the courthouse to the lender, etc., etc. Real estate professionals must add value to the home buying and selling process. They must be able to counsel and advise the buyer about all the dimensions and nuances of the property and all the ramifications of the decision to buy *this* house. They must be able to design a marketing strategy for the seller that specifically targets the population groups most likely to purchase *that* house. They must be able to offer the principals in the transaction the swiftest and most trouble-free route to settlement.

All this requires a new type of business model. The model is different in that it is a major departure from how real estate professionals are accustomed to doing business. **It is a model that is less face-to-face and people intensive than the current model.** It is a transaction management model rather than the gateway model. Technology will be used to automate the routine parts of the transaction—mortgage loan application, title search, document transfer, appointment arrangements—and delegate them to clerical level personnel.

This is, of course, the transactions management model we discussed in Chapter 1. In that model, the real estate professional took charge of doing or arranging for all aspects of the transaction—from search or listing to the last signature on the settlement sheet—and became the indispensable resource for the consumer. The use of the power of one is an enabler for the real estate professional to assume this role of the transaction manager.

The professional will concentrate on the parts of the transaction that require expertise and experience. The real value that seasoned real estate professionals can bring to the marketplace is through counseling and negotiation. The professional will also work intensively with databases available on the Net to make the buyer's and the seller's searches more efficient and faster.

Service needs to be personalized to the level of one. There is a portion of the real estate industry that has already discovered how to do this. The most successful agents, the top producers, have begun to develop their own mini-firms. Either by using technology, or though the use of personal assistants, they are extending their reach far beyond their powers as an individual. They remain inside brokerages, largely owing to state licensing law requirements, but operate in a way much larger than themselves.

Brokers need to discover this as well. Right now, they have little control over their name (see Chapter 7, "Sell the experience, not the product"). Using the power of one can mean creating a system that allows every one of their agents to be the equivalent of the firm. This involves both a capital and training commitment to make the firm operate under a standardized practice, but also involves the enforcement of a discipline that makes every agent operate in the same way. The challenge here is to alter an agent culture that values independence.

FIGURE 2.5   Technology Changes the Transaction (New System)

Technology Changes the Transaction
New System

🕐   Consumers have more control over transaction.

🕐   Settlement providers have attained more of a role in the transaction.

🕐   Information is democratized, but is it relevant or meaningful?

🕐   Realtors must turn information into knowledge and add value to the transaction.

🕐   This can be done by creating a "One Stop Shopping" transaction utilizing the Digital Channel.

Source: John Tuccillo

A NEW APPROACH TO LISTING HOMES

But just as the Net presents a challenge, it also offers solutions. Most specifically, it allows the real estate professional to refashion the listing process into one that is more attractive to the consumer than any other, and uses the Net to fully meet the needs and desires of customers (see Figure 2.5). And the most interesting thing here is that it can build off the old model. Under the old model, the consumer is accustomed to go to the real estate office first when beginning the buying and selling process. When they come to the real estate practitioner and find a modern approach to marketing, they will go no further.

Think about the value the real estate professional can bring to the listing side of the transaction by using the Net. That listing can be targeted to specific buyer groups that represent the most likely buyers, reducing time on the market and increasing the sales price. This gives the consumer time and reduces stress, both of which add significant value and command compensation.

The targeting is done by creating a profile of the consumers who have purchased similar houses. Using office and MLS sales data, the real estate professional can match sales to buyers and create a picture of the household most likely to buy. The profile can then be matched against Census data and other related databases to identify the location of the most likely buyers. Other relational databases add details to the picture (such as income, family size, consumption patterns), allowing a full marketing plan to be developed. Now the print and electronic advertising designed to sell the house will be closely targeted only to the markets that will produce the quickest and most effective sale. With sufficient information, even high probability buyers who are relocating into an area can be profiled and targeted.

The manner in which this can be done is difficult and costly, but ultimately it is necessary to meet the competition technology is spawning. In later chapters, we describe this process, called data mining, in more detail. For now, though, it's sufficient to know that the power of one works for the real estate professional in creating value.

HOW CAN I USE THIS RULE?

There is a hierarchy of understanding that has bearing here.

- **Data** are individual pieces of information, like "the sun rises in the East." These are the basic building blocks of understanding, but they don't create much in the way of value.
- **Information** is the accumulation of facts, like "the sun rises in the East and sets in the West." Information helps understanding and provides value to those who don't have the information. If the information is highly accessible (like the examples above), its value to the recipient is small to none. Because information about real estate was historically not very accessible to the layman, it had great value, and that value accrued to the bearer of the information.
- **Knowledge** is information that is actionable, information that allows the individual to take actions that yield value. So, "If you are lost in the woods, you can tell direction by looking to the sun" is potentially life-saving and is considerably more valuable than simple information.
- The final stage of the hierarchy is **wisdom** ("Don't go into the woods") which requires no explanation, but represents strong insight.

Real estate professionals have traditionally operated on the first two levels of this hierarchy—data and information—in the market and were compensated for conveying data and information from point A to point B. The power of one has stripped the market value from that occupation. Value is created now only by turning information into knowledge. The information that real estate professionals possess is immense, but they are not accustomed to turning that information into knowledge. It was sufficient to sell information to customers. But now the bar has been raised and value can only come from knowledge *creation.* In other words, real estate professionals have to move up the hierarchy and operate on the third and fourth levels—knowledge and wisdom. Only these will command compensation in the new real estate market.

For the real estate industry, this presents a real challenge. Under current business models, all information flows through some intermediary in the marketplace: REALTOR®, mortgage banker, relocation firm, etc. Now, much of the information and analysis of the real estate market can be done by the individual prior to any contact. This will inevitably alter compensation patterns and thus the way in which the business is organized. *The lesson here is that you need to recognize the enhanced economic power of the individual and accommodate it within your business model.* Become your own Wizard of Oz!

The bottom line is that you need to see how the changes in the real estate model are altering the relationships between you and your customers and competition, then use technology to wield the power of one in your market, creating a consistent and satisfying experience for your customers (Chapter 7). The power of one is enhanced if you maximize your content (Chapter 5) and then use data mining (Chapter 6) to bind your customer to you for life (Chapter 3).

2

Lock the Customer In for Life by Creating Unique Value

Trying to increase your market share means selling as much of your product as you can to as many customers as you can. Driving for share of customer, on the other hand, means ensuring that each individual customer who buys your product buys more product, buys only your brand of product and is happy using your product instead of some other type of product as a solution to his problem.[1]

–Don Peppers and Martha Rogers, *The One to One Future*, p. 18

ADVENTURES IN RETAIL

One of the hardest things to find in the marketplace—especially for women—is a pair of jeans that fit correctly. Any manufacturer who can pull off the feat of creating such a pair of jeans would enlist the loyalty of customers forever. Levi's has evidently mastered this. Using database management and computerized production, it offers the customer form-fitted jeans, made to order in a relatively short period. The result delighted consumers, obviously.

Other companies can match Levi's innovation—the technology is not all that complex. But Levi's will probably still retain that customer's loyalty. Using any other company will subject the customer to repeat measurement and the loss of time. Why do all that again, when Levi's already has them on file? Levi's has begun the process of locking the customer in for life.

---

[1] From *The One to One Future* by Don Peppers and Martha Rogers, Ph.D. Copyright ©1993 by Don Peppers and Martha Rogers, Ph.D. Used by permission of Doubleday, a division of Random House,Inc.

ADVENTURES IN HOSPITALITY

Recently, the *Wall Street Journal* reported that Harrah's, the hotel and casino operator, was building a database from the expenditures of its customers augmented by other relational databases. (A relational database consist of information on individuals related by a universal identifier, like Social Security number, address, telephone number, etc. Market research professionals use it to target households.) Creating that would allow Harrah's to chart all their customers' tastes and thus be able to create a perfect experience for them every time they visited the hotel or casino. This database would include not only food and room preferences, but also gaming results and any comments passed on by the guest in the course of a visit. Moreover, other databases containing demographic and economic data would be linked to Harrah's so that as complete a picture as possible might be drawn of the guest. When the guest arrives, there are no questions or delays. Every repeat visitor can hit Vegas much as Michael Corleone did.

The Ritz Carlton chain is renowned for service. In fact, it's even won a Baldrige award for quality, the first service firm to do so. Part of the secret of the Ritz is the empowerment of its employees. Each worker is expected to solve any guest's problem instantly, and can commit up to $1,000 of the company's money to do so. But more important is the memory of the Ritz. If you order a glass of wine from room service and ask for ice, you will be asked about the ice whenever you order wine at any Ritz.

Marriott has recently begun experimenting with precision room service. If you order room service breakfast for 6:30 a.m., it will probably arrive between 6:20 and 6:40. And you're not surprised. Marriott can now deliver that breakfast perfectly ready to eat at precisely 6:30. Stay at the Marriott a couple of times and you *will* be surprised (and a bit annoyed) when the meal shows up a little late.

ADVENTURES IN SOFTWARE

When Netscape released its Navigator software, it did so before the program was perfected (see Chapter 1), because it saw the need to beat everyone else to the market if they were to become the standard for Internet browsing. When it mailed out 40 million copies of Navigator when the software was not complete, Netscape told the recipients that the software was not free of bugs. But it invited its customers to suggest improvement, in effect partnering with Netscape to create the final product.

For the most part, consumers took the invitation seriously, and forwarded their suggestions. With 40 million copies on the street, the odds are that any given suggestion was received hundreds of thousands of times. Yet, whenever an improvement appeared in a later version of the browser, some customers out there saw their ideas in practice, and proudly told their friends and neighbors. This bound the customer more closely to the company and the product (at least until Microsoft wore Netscape down).

ADVENTURES AT THE SUPERMARKET

Publix is a super market chain that operates throughout Florida. It has a reputation for personalized customer service, largely because it carefully compiles extensive records on its clients. Like other chains, Publix offers a customer card, ostensibly designed to offer discounts on selected products. When a customer enters the checkout station, the clerk scans the card and thus opens the computer file of that customer. As goods pass over the scanner a complete purchase record is established. This builds a profile of the customer's habits, and, when connected to relational databases that deal with income and family type, creates a complete socioeconomic profile of the customer.

The information is used in two ways. As a superb marketing database, the Publix records have market value. But more importantly, the data allow Publix to carefully target consumers for promotions, coupons and discounts. Now, regular customers receive packets in the mail that they can actually use, for products they actually buy! Like the Marriott breakfast service, the second time it happens, you realize it's no fluke, and the competition has a new standard to follow.

The examples could go on and on. Next time you call Lands' End, L. L. Bean and similar catalogue "stores," notice how you're greeted and any suggestion the customer representative makes about goods that might interest you. The odds are, he or she is looking at your record and matching it with items currently on sale.

THE NAME OF THE GAME

Each of these companies is involved in essentially the same process. As the world offers more and more choice, it becomes increasingly difficult to create customer loyalty. Doing so in this techno-savvy, consumer-centric world requires becoming the *only* choice for the consumer. Creating a bond that is difficult to break is the method of choice. Whenever a company can provide continuously delightful service combined with a quality product, they will come. Whenever the consumer finds it difficult, costly or impossible to recreate the satisfying and positive experience with another supplier, she will always come back to the company who "knows" her.

Technology allows this to happen. Marriott can bring the breakfast hot and on time by using expert systems that guide the cooks and waitstaff through a series of steps that will produce the desired result. Linking telephone and computer systems allows the L. L. Bean clerk to appear to be your oldest and best friend. Relational databases plus scanning technology allows Publix to create specific packages for its customers.

Customer differentiation is not new. Commercial banks, to cite one example, have long used the prime rate as a concession to their best customers, establishing preferential lending rates to attract and lock in depositors and borrowers who represented high levels of profit to the bank. This "customer relationship" set up a cost-benefit equation that dictated how much in concessions the bank would offer to keep the customer. Currently, relationship banking is the operating mode for commercial banks. And, before Harrah's approach to relational databases, casinos in Las Vegas would "comp" their best players (losers) with rooms, food and credit.

So there are no secrets here. Some companies have been on the lending edge in applying technology to the challenge of locking in the customer in a world where the choices are baffling to the buyer and dangerous to the vendor. But basically all the marketers use similar systems in order to establish a customer familiarity that creates and sustains brand loyalty. Their approach centers around three pieces, which collectively are termed "one-to-one marketing":

- Identify your customers
- Link their identities to their transactions with you
- Ask your customers about their business with your competitors

The key lies in attracting the customers in the first place and having a system that will keep them with you. Ultimately, you want to change the way in which your customers think and the expectations they carry with them into the market. Right now they look out at all their choices and pick one based on any number of reasons. You want them to think of you first and pick another only if it is superior to what they *know* you can offer them.

The examples above show firms that have created a customer relationship that makes consumers feel that their needs are being met exactly and superbly. The service is "mass customized," a powerful bond with the consumer. Mass customization in effect moves customers along the learning curve. Any competitor could match the process. They could replicate the process and effort exactly, and still not win the customer. Put simply, consumers don't necessarily want to undergo the additional cost to work with other companies to build a *second* personal profile. Since the customer has gone to some effort to provide data to one company, duplicating this data means sustaining the same costs. In other words, successful marketing creates a competitive edge and sets up a barrier to competition.

ADVENTURES IN REAL ESTATE?

The need to create a one-to-one marketing system is no less important in the real estate business. The industry is even more exposed now in the marketing area. The power of one has given the consumer more leverage in the real estate transaction, and other competitors have entered the market. From mortgage bankers to Microsoft, the consumer now has a myriad of choices to accomplish the transaction. It's easy to say that the consumer will not abandon the real estate licensee because of tradition. It's more accurate to say that consumer loyalty in the real estate market is up for grabs and is not given automatically to anyone.

For the real estate professional, the key to the future is value added, which translates to excellence, innovation, and anticipation. This future is reached through strategies that emphasize understanding, identifying, attracting, serving and retaining "customers for life." The approaches described above are extremely valuable to the real estate agent and broker.

There is, however, a major barrier for the industry. In all the examples described above, customers visit frequently. (Even in the case of Harrah's, regular players can be expected to stay at the hotel upwards of four times a year.) Real estate suffers from the fact that sales are made infrequently. The best customers show up no more than every three years. The creation and development of customer loyalty cannot be helped by often-repeated contacts.

The saving grace here is that in most cases, the real estate business is developed by referral—through friends, family or other firms. Equally important is the network of professional contacts (either formal or informal) that send business from one firm to another across the country. Those referrals can come more frequently if the real estate firm is able to customize each transaction so that it can only have taken place for that particular individual. Using mass customization can create that reputation.

CREATING THE MARKETING MODEL

Real estate professionals need to figure out what this means for them and implement their own system. There are four steps in this process: (1) find out as much as you can about your customers; (2) evaluate the worth of each customer to your overall operation; (3) make the transaction a completely satisfying experience; and (4) identify your service as distinctly better than that of your competition.

1. *Learn all you can about your customers and their needs.* The first step is clearly psychographics: who is the customer in terms of income, location, ethnicity, net worth and buying habits? The place to start is in your own files. As we described in Chapter 2, real estate agents and firms have within their files a mountain of information about closed transactions

and buyer applications. These contain the raw materials necessary to create customer files similar to the information that Publix collects through its scanners.

Translating this information into a useable form is a challenge, since real estate professionals are not normally at ease with database creation and data analysis, and most firms do not have the staff necessary to do this task. So the creation of customer profiles should be outsourced. An excellent and cost-effective way of doing this is to visit the local university or junior college and find a faculty member or student who will turn your raw data into a coherent, useable database. In all probability, this can be done in an economical manner.

When you do this, be sure to ask about how to tie your records into both the MLS data for your market and other relational databases (census, market research information, etc.) This is the resource that will allow you to seize the power of one to lock in your customer. In the end, you should have a complete picture of not only your own customer base, but also profiles of *prospective* customers.

2. *Assess the total value of each customer.* Although it is culturally difficult for real estate practitioners to believe, some customers are more valuable than others are. Households who move often, those who are opinion leaders in the community or have wide networks of family and friends will generate more income than others who do not share these characteristics.

    If you are recoiling from this thought as either unfair or discriminatory, think about relocation firms and affinity programs. We seek these out and ally with them because they are a rich source of business. Real estate professionals and firms also create informal networks among themselves for the purposes of generating referrals. And while these networks may be based on a variety of other factors, we tend to gravitate toward those who offer the most potential benefit. The better the source, the more highly we value it. In fact, most agents and firms will pay a significant portion of their commission income to a referral source to maintain the relationship.

The real estate firm must evaluate each customer on the basis of the psychographic profile developed from historical data. The evaluation is done on as individual a basis as possible. The data cannot be used to make gross generalizations. Rather, the analysis will indicate the degree to which the real estate agent will "bid" to capture a larger share of a given customer's business.

The bidding can be done in the form of lower commissions, additional services or simply a closer relationship. Moreover, the relationship would carry over beyond the specific transaction, to the point where customers would think of you and you only when the topic of real estate pops into their heads.

3. *Create a system that makes the transaction a completely satisfying experience.* We deal with this topic more extensively in Chapter 7, "Sell the Experience, Not the Product," which deals with the operation of such a system. The key to any of this is understanding what the consumer sees as costs in the transaction process. The quick and obvious answer is to look at the settlement sheet. There, the largest items are the real estate commission and the fees associated with financing.

The reality is that the consumer sees time and stress as the largest costs of the process. Buying a house is an intellectual decision that can be made in the cool rationality of the kitchen table. Buying *this* house is an emotional process. Under current condi-

T • • • • •
he current issue of affinity fees, whereby various groups are asserting their rights to a large portion of the real estate commission simply because of who they are, is a manifestation of the importance of referral to the real estate professional. It couldn't be done if the practitioners did not value customers differently. The argument in this chapter is essentially that this problem will go away if the real estate agent or firm can lock in its own customers the way the firms described earlier can.   • • • • •

tions, the rush the consumer gets when she finds the "dream house" is diluted and diminished between that moment and the moment three months later when she actually takes possession. That gap is a real cost.

Consumer surveys consistently place the home transaction among the top five stressful events for most people. During the time of the transaction, uncertainty weighs heavily on both buyer and seller. Questions about financing, appraisal, home inspection and title hang in the air until the last document is signed and the title conveys. This is also a real cost to the consumer, and is manifest in the degree of stress related to the home buying and selling process.

The service system you offer consumers must be directed to reducing these costs. Part of this is to set up a process that cuts the time of the transaction (see Chapter 7). Part of it consists of offering a package of service that sets up a "one-stop shopping" experience for the consumer. The degree to which you value your customer will determine how far you go in this direction.

4. *Differentiate your service from that of your competitors.* Real estate professionals have traditionally attempted to do this in one of three ways.

   a. promotional gifts (how many calendars can one really use?) designed to keep the name of the agent in clear and constant sight. This is basically a hit–or–miss proposition. Either the household keeps the gift or throws it away. Even when it keeps the gift, there's no assurance that this household will be in the market that year.

   b. advertise success. The newspaper ads citing listed or closed volume and bearing the agent's high school graduation picture are the prime examples of this. The hope is that the consumer will be attracted to someone prominent in the market. The danger, of course, is that the consumer figures that these agents are too busy to give them the individual attention they need.

   c. farming tools like postcards to put their name in front of the public. Most often, these are tossed like the cents-off coupons sent by most supermarkets. This method works if the farming tools are crafted the way Publix crafts its coupon mailings.

   True differentiation of services requires the delivery of real value to the consuming public. Statistics indicate that the choice of a real estate agent is most often the result of some personal relationship. A friend, a relative, a colleague has had a satisfying experience with a particular real estate professional and urges others to use that agent's services. If you can reduce stress and give back time, you will differentiate yourself from the pack.

THE ISSUE OF TIME

Repeat buyers have different behaviors in different markets. For a newsstand, it ought to be a daily visit. For a supermarket, it is perhaps a weekly occurrence. At a hotel, quarterly visits may constitute frequent patronage. But for a real estate company, repeat business may come only at three- to seven-year intervals. That frequency makes it extremely difficult to lock a customer in—in fact, it may make it impossible.

It is important in this process for real estate professionals to figure a way to "increase" that frequency to allow for the creation of customers for life. Obviously, passing some sort of law requiring that households move every year and use a real estate licensee in the process would solve the problem. Too bad that can't be done!

COLLABORATE WITH THE CUSTOMER

There are two answers to this dilemma and they work in concert. The first is to create a *collaborative marketing relationship* with your customers. Collaborative marketing occurs when you listen as your customer speaks, and when you invite your customer to participate in actually making the product before asking the customer to take it (like Netscape).

What does this mean in real estate? It means developing an extensive feedback loop with your customers during and after the transaction. Some firms have consumer satisfaction surveys, but these are designed primarily to create advertising claims. Most of us get a survey after we have our cars serviced. Usually, it's accompanied by a letter saying that unless we rate all aspects of the dealership as a "10," the service manager will be publicly flogged. Hardly, but those "10" ratings are displayed proudly in the service office.

The problem with these surveys is that they reveal only what they ask. Were you greeted courteously? Was your car ready when promised? Etc. None of this means a great deal and none of it allows the customer (except with great effort) to enter a dialogue with the deliverer of the service. With no real dialogue, there is no learning, and the next customer gets the same service—both level and type—as the last one. More importantly, the customer expects that no learning will occur and will go anywhere she feels like the next time around. No customer loyalty has been created.

You need to do better than that. You need to create a learning experience with your customers that makes you a better real estate professional and leaves your clients with the impression that you will tailor your services to each and every individual with whom you work.

A couple of weeks after the transaction (giving them time to settle in), visit your customers in their new home. Use the visit to explain to them that you'd like to become the real estate professional of choice for everyone in your market area and, in that regard, you'd like their help. Then review the transaction, item by item, asking what could have been done differently to better meet their needs. Now extend the question by asking them to think about their friends and family, including people of all ages. How could the transaction have been tailored to fit their needs and wants?

Wrap up the interview by asking them to keep in touch and to let you know if they see anything in the marketplace that could help you reach your goal. I guarantee you that this interview will be appreciated and valued more than the plant on the doorstep or the annual calendar.

By implementing this process, you have created what the technologists refer to as an "expert system," a computer program designed to accumulate experience and bring it to bear on questions of interest. Marriott uses expert systems to created the perfect on-time breakfast described above.

You are doing so without electronic help, but are repeating the process that has proven so helpful in cementing customer loyalty. And using expert systems substitutes knowledge for often-repeated transactions.

AND HIS SISTERS AND HIS COUSINS AND HIS AUNTS

The second method of overcoming the problem of infrequent real estate dealings is to *look at each customer as an extended unit*. Surveys by the National Association of REALTORS® have consistently indicated that the most frequent factor in the choice of a real estate professional or firm is word of mouth. Either a friend, relative or colleague recommends the use of a particular licensee and the consumer follows.

The reasons for these recommendations vary and are not all tied to excellence of service. It may be that the recommender is a neighbor of the agent, or goes to the same church. That's usually OK because the real estate industry has not consciously built up a reputation for the kind of service delivered by, say, Ritz Carlton, so the choice really doesn't matter.

Remember, the old real estate gatekeeper model (see Chapter 1) has the public coming to anyone who has the most familiar acquaintance with information about the market. When Alice encounters the Cheshire Cat at a crossroads and asks which road to take, the cat asks about her destination. When she says she has none, he replies that any road will get her there. So, too, with the real estate market: any agent will get you there and since you won't come back for seven years, even bad service is acceptable.

Break that cycle. If you can develop the system of expert, excellent, customized service described above, you will break the mold, just as Marriott is breaking the "sort of on time" breakfast service experience. Consumers can be brought about to the expectation of excellent service by your practice. When that occurs, your competition will look lost and ineffective by comparison.

Because word of mouth is the primary method of communication in the real estate market, you can raise consumer expectations with even a few transactions done under the system. Real estate is a great cocktail party chatter subject. The fact that you've created a personalized system of service and then checked back with your customers to get their help in becoming even better will make your name part of every one of those conversations.

Now, recommending the casual acquaintance to the prospective buyer or seller will no longer be good enough when there is an alternative in the market that is clearly superior. Of course, this is what's done now. The top producers deliver the best service in the marketplace. That's how they have achieved their position, and each one has their own system, usually created from the ideas of the many education seminars they attend. Word of mouth recommendation is based on that service.

By creating a system of excellent and personalized service, any real estate professional can develop the same kind of reputation. The system described above can make each customer feel that the agent is working only for them— just as the top producer makes her customers feel. Any firm that introduces such a system for its agents will be the firm of choice in the marketplace.

SHIFTING GEARS: A ONE-TO-ONE MARKETING STORY

You've probably never heard of Laura Herring, although her business touches real estate. Ms. Herring was trained as a clinical psychologist and created a small practice serving business through employee assistance programs. As these grew in the Seventies and Eighties, she came into contact with more and more executives. As she listened to them, she realized that the companies they worked for could use some analysis. She migrated her practice to executive training, handling topics from personal initiative to creativity to coaching executive spouses. In this last area, again by listening to the client, she discovered that the traumas of relocation were a major problem. From this she created a self-help course and proceeded to sell it (laboriously) to corporate America.

Eventually the course caught on, and the clients who used it supplied her with other business ideas. Community research enabled her to give her customers a product that would overcome the information barriers that existed in relocation—finding child and elder care, schools, etc. Soon other products followed: counseling for employees reluctant to relocate, outplacement for accompanying spouses and even recruitment services.

The secret to this success is the ability to listen and to exchange information. Her clients point to the fact that everyone on her staff listens constantly and asks the customers what they need. Within the staff, idea and information exchange is a key component of the culture. The lesson here is directly applicable to the real estate firm, both in the way in which the customer is brought into the product development process and in the willingness to follow the customer's lead in entering new business lines.

BUT EVERYONE WILL DO IT!

The history of the real estate industry is that innovators are followed slavishly. If a firm innovates its service in its market, all the others will follow with a variation very quickly. The national example of this is how Re/Max, skillfully adapting an idea pioneered by Realty Executives, pushed the entire industry into accepting and using the 100 percent concept in one form or another.

So, how can you follow this rule to its application without being drowned out in a din of competition? The answer is speed. The industry has not yet adapted fully to general rule #1 (Speed Kills). Rather, when an innovation comes along, the industry will stand on the sidelines and see how it works in the market. It's almost like the people watching the first guy who ate a lobster ("He looks like he's enjoying it, but let's wait to see if he dies").

Assume you are the first agent or firm in your market to develop and implement a complete service system that can be customized and to collaborate with your customers to improve that system on a continuous basis. Your competitors will wait to see if your new approach works. By the time they are satisfied that it will, your reputation and word of mouth recommendations will have established you as the front runner and innovator. Think back to Re/Max. No matter how often the 100 percent concept is used by others, it's still identified with them. That's a significant marketplace edge.

HOW CAN I USE THIS RULE?

After you read and understand this chapter, take some time and review your customer files and your service offerings.

On the data side:

- Use the information in the files to create some customer profiles that will allow you to evaluate the value of each customer to you.
- Extend this to the files in your firm and the description of closed sales on the MLS.

- Hire a graduate student who can crunch these numbers and relate them to the other databases that might be publicly available.

On the service side:

- Figure how you can reduce the time and stress of the transaction for the consumer.
- Investigate the various online links that will connect you to other settlement service providers.
- Establish a feedback system to let customers help you to improve your service.

The bottom line here is that if you can bind the customer to you for life, you will prosper in the new world of the real estate business. Seize the power of one (Rule #1) and use technology to mine your bits (Rule #5), creating a business where you sell the experience—not the product (Rule #6).

The Middle Is Disappearing

Unlike tomatoes or cars, real estate listings, stock quotations and airline schedules are bits, easily and inexpensively shipped at the speed of light. Bits need no warehousing, and the cost to make more is effectively zero. For this reason, real estate agents, stockbrokers and travel agents will disappear much more rapidly than food wholesalers or car dealers.[1]

–Nicholas Negroponte, *WiReD*, September 1997.

REMEMBER WHEN BEING A BANK OFFICER MEANT SOMETHING?

In *Death of a Salesman*, Willy Loman is forced to face an avalanche of reality. One of the truths in that mass is his redundancy as a salesman. Younger people using different business methods and newer technology–although in this case, it's just the telephone–have replaced him. In modern terms, Willy is a middleman, and his world has less use for middlemen. Like most people, he takes it hard, ultimately committing suicide.

Few react as violently, but change is hard. It has never been harder than with the disappearance of the middle– the "glue" of the American experience. So, too, the recent history of the United States has been characterized by the disappearance of the middle. It seems that in every aspect of our existence, there is less of the middle. The election of 1994 shifted control of the Congress from the Demo-

---

[1] Article by Nicholas Negroponte appeared in WiReD, September, 1997, p. 208. Reprinted with permission of the author.

crats to the Republicans. Yet, while conservative Republicans won that majority, it was not at the expense of the most liberal Democrats. Rather, moderates of both parties lost. Not only was the party makeup of the Congress changed, so too was the ideological climate. Debate was now more polarized, positions hardened and productive legislation (assuming that the phrase is not an oxymoron) harder to pass.

The social fabric appears polarized as well. Responses to questions of health, lifestyle, education and personal behavior all seem to lie on the ends of the spectrum. Violence, once all fists and rocks, is now more often bullets and explosives.

The middle of the economy is also disappearing. The recession of 1990-91, as a case in point, began in the financial services industry when all the fine young vice presidents were revealed to be nothing more than white collar burger-flippers. Their function had been to take information from point A and carry it to point B without augmenting it in any real way. Their function—such as it was—could be done more efficiently and more cheaply by computer.

INCOME DISPARITY GROWS . . . AND THE MIDDLE SHRINKS

Income distribution has widened, as well. Statistics suggest that the income gains during the Nineties have accrued disproportionately to those in the upper ten percent of the income distribution, with the middle-income ranges actually losing wages over the past ten years. The movement to a knowledge-based economy from a manufacturing economy has created jobs, but they increasingly demand technological sophistication. So, for those who are technologically savvy, the economy offers significant rewards.

Relative Income Changes: 1989-1998 (First Half)

Income Decile	Percentage Change In Hourly Wages
Lowest 10%	+6.0%
Second 10%	+2.8%
Third 10%	0
Fourth 10%	0
Fifth 10%	−1.2%
Sixth 10%	−1.4%
Seventh 10%	−1.7%
Eighth 10%	0
Ninth 10%	+4.0%
Highest 10%	n.a.

Source: U.S. Department of Commerce

For others, the path to success and wealth is less clear: there are a series of jobs which may pay decently and require little in the way of technical skills, but no real careers. There is nothing in between. Contrast this to the Fifties (Willy Loman-time?) when the postwar economic boom was built on the bedrock of steady, middle class, blue collar, mostly unionized jobs.

Those jobs contributed to the strength of middle class, stable neighborhoods, where role models abounded and kids grew up wanting to be like Uncle Joe, not like Mike.

The discrepancy today between haves and have-nots is not just in income; it's also in the social environment in which each lives. Now we are creating jobs of great potential but little social importance (that pay very well), or pay very little because they are unskilled or semi-skilled.

Manufacturing jobs that create middle class homes and middle class households are declining as a percentage of all jobs, and declining with them is the economic middle. What "middle class jobs" we create are often dispersed and clearly not conducive to a restoration of community.

This disappearance of the middle also hits home to specific businesses. Sears was traditionally identified with middle America. It has struggled to recreate itself because its market has disappeared. This is difficult because the competition has boxed it in. On the upscale side, high-touch companies like Nordstrom have cut off the affluent market. Shoppers looking for quality and price will immediately identify those characteristics with Nordstrom. Below the middle class, Wal-Mart has established a price and service proposition that has taken away the lower income market. Both Nordstrom and Wal-Mart, by the way, have locked their customers in by creating a unique identity that carries with it value for the consumer (see Chapter 3).

THE INTERNET MAKES IT EASIER

There is another manifestation of this disappearance of the middle. In this case, the traditional economic intermediary is vanishing and being replaced by newer incarnations. The savings and loan crisis of the Eighties was generated in part by changes in financial markets that resulted in a wider variety of choice that could be directly accessed by consumers. Mutual funds, ESOPs, stock reinvestment plans, and other channels reduced the attractiveness of bank deposits. As consumers left the fold, the thrift industry business model of borrow short and lend long began to collapse.

Consumers now place their wealth in a variety of instruments—401(k) plans, life insurance, pension funds, stocks and bonds—which allow them to ride the prosperity of this economy. The intermediaries consumers deal with are no longer the banks. They might be the human resource professional who administers the company pension plan. Even mortgages have become another form of financial instrument with the consumer having the ability to adjust his housing equity by prepaying or borrowing more, often through finance companies rather than banks.

The point here is that an entire industry disappeared because consumers had the ability to invest their money for an adequate return without needing to go through a bank. The benefits of a disappearing middle to the consumer are obvious: if we can deal directly with suppliers, the markup in the price of goods that accrues to the intermediary goes away. So peaches would cost 75 cents a pound instead of a dollar. Clearly there are areas—especially where preparation and packaging are involved—where the middleman remains necessary, but there are many areas where the disappearing middle is an absolute boon to the consumer.

The Internet has extended this principle to a much wider range of goods and services. The story of virtual vineyards discussed earlier is another example of how and why the middle of the transaction disappears. The problem faced by microwineries is the physical distance between them and their markets and the wide dispersion of the market. The Internet allows for a consolidation of the market and a single channel for reaching it. It creates a virtual marketplace.

The change in how transactions occur because of the Internet and electronic commerce has public policy ramifications as well. Money has always served as a substitute for information in the marketplace. The role of the government in issuing money is to provide assurance that value is being given for value received. The Internet removes the information gaps in the market and thus makes money less and less necessary. How then will Alan Greenspan and the Federal Reserve control monetary policy in a world where money is less necessary and useful? To date, the Fed has adapted well and appears to have a handle on this particular evolution. But watch this as it unfolds; it will have significant ramifications for everyone who is involved in any kind of transaction.

So it is in a variety of other areas. Pick a good or service that is independent of physical presence and it's likely that the proliferation of the Internet has changed its market dramatically. Let's look at four of them:

1. *Books* can be judged interesting or not on the basis of reviews in the newspaper. In addition, we generally restrict our reading to particular categories—fiction, business, history, etc.—so we don't need to look extensively. The Book of the Month Club and its clones seized upon this fact to create a market niche, but never dislodged the booksellers. Here comes the Internet and Amazon.com, an unlimited virtual store. Amazon can provide you not only with any book in print at a discount, but also reviews of the book and (locking the customer in with the power of one again) related books which your buying habits suggest would interest you.

    The results have been extraordinary, to the point where profits of major book chains have declined. Barnes and Noble, a traditional bookseller, has even opened a copycat site to compete in the cybermarket. Of course, smaller bookstores remain because there is still utility in being able to browse and feel the books. But the chains who have been successful in holding the middle, primarily Borders and Barnes and Noble, have done so by transforming themselves into multipurpose entertainment centers, with coffeehouses and live music. More on this later.

2. *Travel agents* have been especially hard hit by the disintermediation of the Internet. Their industry was built on a model of almost pure information brokerage. The agents had access to the major flight and hotel systems and they could offer the public something that it could not get by itself—at least not without extreme cost and effort. The airline guides provided some of this information to the public, but the travel agents had the ability to complete the transaction while accessing the information, something which was beyond the scope of the individual and which was costly.

   The Internet brought the travel information directly into the hands of the public. The movement was begun by the airlines, initially by providing proprietary software to their best customers. They acted from a double motivation: dealing directly with the public eliminated the need to pay commissions to travel agents, and offering customers a valuable tool locked in their loyalty.

   The Internet has transcended this proprietary effort, and there is a variety of travel sites available to the public, led by Microsoft's entry, Expedia. The Internet works for travel because transportation and lodging are commodities: a flight is a flight, a hotel room is a hotel room. Decisions are based on price and convenience. The information intermediation offered by the travel industry has no more value to the public. Consequently, travel industry business is off by 30 to 40 percent. Some firms have adapted, and they are surviving. Again, more on that later.

3. *Insurance agents* offered a different sort of information. Rather than just offering information that was beyond the access of the public (which they did), they also offered an analysis that allowed individuals to customize their coverage. The agent in this

case added value to the purchase of a good that was as much a commodity as travel services. In fact, this service was sufficiently valued by the customer that it served as a differentiator among the various companies in the industry.

The Internet has entered this world as well. Initially, it provided a direct communications link between the individual and the company. When the product desired was simple, like term life insurance, the customer could buy it directly from the company alone in the privacy of his own home. In more complicated transactions, the agent was still a player. But now software is available on the Internet that allows the consumer to walk through all the questions he would have with the agent, and then buy the necessary insurance directly from the company.

The agent has been largely cut out by the power conferred on the consumer by the Internet. Agents have responded by broadening their portfolios to bill themselves as financial planners. They are attempting to create value in different ways for their customers. We return to this point later.

4. *Car dealers* made a great deal of their profit from information discrepancies and locational differences. The supply of particular autos is unevenly distributed across the country. The customer who wanted the best deal on a given model would have to acquire the information on the location of that deal and then physically acquire the vehicle. Dealers, tied into international networks, could more easily access both information and the vehicles themselves.

The salesman acted as the direct contact with the customer and brokered the information she sought. (That's a polite way of putting it, of course. We've all had our experiences with car salesmen!) The customer paid a fee for this service in the form of the dealer's price markup.

On the Internet, one can search everywhere simultaneously for any make or model of car desired. More importantly, the customer can purchase the vehicle at prices that contain only the minimum dealer profit. Faced with this prospect, dealers have little choice but to accept the deal offered by the buyer (there's that power of one again!) or see that business walk out the door and into cyberspace. The upshot of this has been the growth of dealerships, so that they can make up in volume what they lose in margin, and so that they can have their own Web site to sell from. Oh, and the number of salesmen has declined. The industry is polarizing and its intermediary function is disappearing. And, by the way, nearly $1 billion worth of vehicles will be sold on the Web in 1998.

In each of these cases, an industry in the middle of a transaction has seen its market shrink. Now, we're not talking about complete extinction. In reality, the decline is less that 40 percent in even the most extreme cases. But, think about what a loss of that magnitude would do to your business. It's a disaster. And that's the way booksellers, travel agents, insurance agents and car salesmen see it. When you can buy insurance and book plane tickets and hotels on the Web, what's the need for insurance salesmen and travel agents? While more exotic transactions require the need of a professional, a large percentage of deals disappear, and with them industry revenues.

REAL ESTATE PROFESSIONALS ARE
MIDDLEMEN, TOO

If we consider the real estate market model described in Chapter 1, all these trends come to roost in the real estate industry. For most of its life, the real estate industry has derived its profits from brokering information about properties for sale. For the seller, it provided a channel for advertising the property to interested buyers. For the buyer, it brought news about the available inventory. While advice and counseling are always part of the service brought to the market by the agent, the main attraction for the consumer was the agent's control of information. Quality was not a differentiating factor in the real estate market, since virtually all agents had access to information.

The information brokerage offered by real estate professionals extended beyond the property. In the gateway model, the public saw the agent as a source of information for all the other services needed in the transaction. A seller relied on the options offered by the agent in preparing the house for showing; the buyer relied on the agent for information about available mortgage lenders, title companies and home inspectors. The agent would offer a number of choices in each area, but these constituted the entire set of options for the consumer. Any other approach would entail additional cost and effort. And the seller was already paying a significant price for the services of the real estate licensee.

THE INDUSTRY STRUCTURE IS FORMED
BY INTERMEDIATION . . .

The information monopoly enjoyed by the real estate practitioner served as a great leveler in the marketplace. If the property information is what drew the public to the real estate office, then the size of the firm did not matter.

A small outfit with access to the MLS was as viable in the marketplace as the large, multi-office firm. If the large firm could offer additional consumer services, that was fine. But it didn't really matter. The large firms could attract more agents because they could support them better. But from the customer's point of view all were equal. Surveys consistently show that the name of the brokerage is a minimal factor in the choice of the consumer in engaging real estate services.

As the industry grew, it reflected this effect. In 1990, there were approximately 120,000 real estate firms in the United States. Of these, about 60 percent had fewer than five sales associates. This was possible because "large" and "small" had little meaning as competitive concepts in a business where all shared the same information monopoly.

. . . AND RESHAPED BY THE INTERNET

Like other information monopolies and intermediary business, real estate is being reshaped by the democratization of information caused by the Internet. Property information is pretty much open to everyone with access to the Internet, either directly or through friends or relatives—and that covers 62.3 million Americans, 32 percent of the adult population.[2] REALTOR.COM carries virtually the entire sales inventory for existing homes on its public Web site, and there are thousands more that cover cities, states and regions of the United States.

That cuts down severely on the ability of the real estate professional to command compensation for brokering information. Carrying property information from the MLS to the

---

[2] Mediamark Research Corporation, quoted in *Real Estate Intelligence Report,* Summer 1998.

buyer or from the seller to the MLS is a rote function that can be done by machine better than by a real estate licensee. Increasingly, consumers will come to the market having scanned the Web and decided on a limited number of houses of interest, or will have prepared their own listing for the home they seek to sell. The intermediary function that was formerly the exclusive province of the real estate professional has disappeared.

Now, size is indeed a factor in surviving, and the middle is untenable. Those 120,000 firms of 1990 have shrunk to about 90,000 and 60 percent are still very small. But large firms (those with more than 50 associates) employ 70 percent of all sales agents. Large firms can offer a "one-stop shopping" alternative that will appeal to consumers' need for speed and convenience. Additionally, they can create a Web presence that will draw the eyeballs of home seekers. Small firms can offer a personalized service that coddles the customer. The midsize firms that succeed and survive are most often associated with a national franchise, making them equivalent to a larger entity.

On top of this, the competition has expanded. The new model of the transaction as a jigsaw puzzle allows into the market a raft of new competitors. Without information monopoly as the key to controlling the market, a wide range of firms will be influential with consumers in **managing** the transaction. The first firms that pop into the head here are those most closely associated with the transaction, like mortgage bankers and title companies. They can do it, but they have their own problems, again related to the collapse of intermediation. In mortgage banking, for example, the number of independent firms has shrunk at the expense of subsidiaries owned by commercial banks and life insurance companies.

In fact, the field is wide open. Microsoft, for example, is attempting to control the standards for property information access, and through that to control the transaction and ultimately the market. Microsoft has no knowledge of the real estate market, and would seem a pale competitor to the experience represented by the firms now in the market. Of course, Microsoft knew nothing of travel or vehicle sales either, and it got into those markets. Size and money count, and Microsoft has both.

The middle is disappearing from the real estate industry. In brokerage firms, mortgage originators, relocation companies and many other real estate service providers, the economies of scale related to information are driving the market into very large, all-purpose, market-share firms and smaller, highly specialized, boutique-type firms. There is nothing on the horizon that will alter that trend.

GROPING AND COPING

The loss of the intermediation business has not been lost on the real estate industry. One of the reactions has been the growth of buyer brokerage. In the old model, the market leverage resided with the seller. It made little or no sense to represent anyone else, either as an agent or a subagent. Now, information is available to all market players and so the **advising** function becomes more valuable to the consumer. Brokerage arrangements on the other side of the market make sense.

Another reaction is the reduction of commissions. A growing number of transactions are carrying discounted commissions, either directly or because of an affinity relationship.[3] Amerinet is attempting to make this a national

---

[3] Jeremy Conaway, president of RECon Intelligence Services, estimates that a third of all transactions carry discounted commissions and predicts the figure will move to 40 percent within the next few years. (*Real Estate Intelligence Report,* Summer 1998, p. 6).

system through its partnership with Costco and a number of independent brokerages throughout the country.[4] This is not new, since commissions have always been negotiable, but is very unusual in the robust market now being enjoyed all over the country. Normally, widespread discounting is used in an attempt to jump start a sluggish real estate market.

With the loss of information intermediation demand, real estate firms are attempting to differentiate themselves as service providers, either through specialized brokerage or price. Perhaps the most obvious strategy in this regard has been adopted by Cendant, the giant holding company that owns the Century 21, ERA and Coldwell Banker brands. Using its wide holdings in consumer services (hotels, car rental agencies, etc.), Cendant is building an integrated system of consumer services, so that a customer who uses one of the real estate names can access discounted services from other Cendant companies. In addition, it is using its relocation, mortgage origination and home improvement companies to present a single source supplier to the customer.

Cendant is not alone in creating an integrated system. All the other franchises and many of the larger independent firms are devising similar approaches to the consumer. They are all attempting to replace the pure information interme-diation function that was the stock-in-trade of the real estate firm with a multi-service approach that will manage the consumer's transaction.

Some firms, however, and many agents are ignoring the change in the business. They are content to see the MLS as the primary tool in attracting customers and are doing little

---

[4] Amerinet recently altered its arrangement with Costco to meet the demands of state regulators in Oregon. Now the system calls for dis-counted commissions rather than rebates to Costco members as was provided in the original conception. (*Real Estate Intelligence Report,* Summer 1998, p.1).

to adapt to the loss of the middle. It can be done for a while—every change takes time to permeate the entire market. Operating on the old model will sustain for a while, but ultimately is a formula for failure.

BUT WHAT CAN WE DO?

I'd like to fall back on the second law of forecasting ("Damned if I know") here, but I can't. There are strategies that will allow the broker or agent to adapt to this rule. In general, your job here is to recreate a meaningful and valuable intermediary role for yourself that will deliver value to your clients as information brokerage did in the past.

1. To begin with, follow general rule #4 and *walk away from your success*. That means giving up the idea that you are an information broker and that the MLS is your most powerful tool in the marketplace. As an information source, the MLS is dead. It has been transcended by the Internet, which is faster, more flexible, and more accurate. Ultimately, the MLS will either evolve into full service data firms (See Chapter 6, "Mine Your Bits") or be absorbed into another company. The proprietary system of information that is the MLS is a relic, and will add nothing of value in the future.

2. Second, *build on your market position and tools*. Although half the MLS may be an inferior information system, the other half of it—the communications and transactions system—is a very valuable tool. It allows real estate professionals to negotiate at speed with a common basis of knowledge. No one else—from Microsoft to the mortgage banker—who may manage the transaction has so powerful a tool. In addition, the public is accustomed (from the old

real estate model) to consult the real estate licensee first when thinking about buying and selling. Until that mentality dies, you have an edge in the market. But the key is to *build* on it, not *sit* on it.

3. Third, *become a knowledge broker*. In reality, real estate professionals have always delivered value by counseling and negotiating. For most buyers and sellers, this is where value lies. Remember that knowledge is actionable information. The new intermediary provides that knowledge. In effect, you used to tell that customer which properties were on the market; now you evaluate for them the properties they are attracted to.

4. Fourth, regardless of how automated you or your firm becomes, *reintermediate through personalized service*. It may seem silly to stress the value of personal service to real estate professionals. After all, isn't that what they do best? Personalized service here doesn't mean the annual calendar or the gift at closing (see Chapter 3). It means learning about your customers and creating the perfect transaction for them.

The reality of real estate is that the middle has not disappeared so much as it has shifted. The challenge is to recreate that valuable middle role that most consumers value, but do it in a way that's relevant to their needs. In the past, that need was information. Now those needs are knowledge, advice and counseling. Recreating an intermediary function will require building around those tasks.

Most of this book has turned on technology, and the disappearance of the middle is largely a function of technological change. But the strategic reaction to the disappearance of the middle hinges less on what gadgets you can manipulate than on your knowledge of your market (see Chapter 2) and your ability to reassert intermediary value by using it.

LEARNING FROM OTHER INDUSTRIES

Real estate is not the only industry to go through this. Virtually every information intermediary and a good number of other service businesses have gone through the same loss of the middle. Each in its own way has adapted to the fact that its core business has been gutted by the information revolution. In these adaptations lie some lessons for the real estate business.

The booksellers were hurt by the emergence of virtual bookstores, so they reacted by broadening their sense of mission. How? They relied upon the fact that physical bookstores carried with them a sense of place and purpose that was different from any other place. The smell and feel of books couldn't be replicated on the computer. The result? Booksellers re-envisioned themselves as gathering places. The case of Borders is most illustrative. The chain consists of large stores that sell music in addition to books, have coffee bars to rival any Starbucks and, in many cases, have live entertainment on weekends. (Amazon has recently copied Borders by adding CDs to its stock.)

Travel agents were hurt by the emergence of travel services on the Internet and lost a considerable portion of their business. Those who survived and prospered did so by adding knowledge to their competencies. Now travel agencies serve as advisors to those clients who want exactly the right itinerary, and the most appropriate accommodations. The successful travel agencies say, "John, if you liked Siena, why not consider spending some time in San Gemignano? I think you'll like that too." They have added knowledge to information.

*B*ut Shouldn't We Fight To Protect Our Information?

The newest buzzword in the real estate industry is "intellectual property." The issue refers to MLS listing information and the question is whether the MLS will retain control over real estate information by copyrighting property data. The National Association of REALTORS® has even made a very effective video alerting the industry to the problem and indicating how this "intellectual property" can be preserved.

The real protagonists in this drama are Real Select, operator of REALTOR.COM, and Microsoft, operator of everything. Real Select currently has the entire inventory (or darn close to it) described on its site, together with a great deal more information of interest and use to consumers. Microsoft has the world's best (and if it beats the Department of Justice, the only) distribution system for information and a ton of money. It is trying to use both of these to lure the information away from REALTOR.COM and onto its own entry in the consumer enticement derby.

If you recognize the disappearance of the middle and the need to reassert the intermediary function, you know that this is the wrong debate and the wrong issue. Focusing on information as "intellectual property" draws the energy and attention away from the more important job of figuring out how to turn information into knowledge to attract consumers to your business.   *(Continued)*

> We are long past the point where the market will pay for the transmission of information. Travel agents, insurance salesmen, bank executives and, to a certain extent, REALTORS®, have all seen how the demand for their own services has declined as information falls in price and increases in accessibility. Information is now freely available to everyone; it is more powerful if shared than if hoarded. Daniel Burrus, the technology guru, uses an apt metaphor. If one enters a darkened room with a lit candle, the room becomes brighter. You can then light every candle in the room, but your candle is undiminished. And when you have finished, the room is filled with the brightness of all the candles. Information sharing is like that. • • • • •

Insurance agents have been sliced and diced by the ability of consumers to buy insurance electronically. Once again, those agents who survived have done so by redefining their business. Increasingly, insurance agents are selling themselves as financial planners (which, of course, sits badly with professional financial planners). This evolution is interesting both because the insurance people have broadened their operational scope and because their new positioning fits the aging of the baby–boom generation perfectly. More and more Americans are appreciating the value of financial planning and see its application to them.

Finally, car salesmen face direct competition from the Internet, which has eroded their information and geographic leverage. The reaction of the more progressive (and aggressive) dealers has been to face the competition directly by selling over the Internet. Large dealers have gotten larger and increased their volume to cover smaller margins.

Each of these sounds a great deal like real estate. But the lessons are instructive. Like booksellers and insurance agents, real estate firms can broaden the definition of their business to include all aspects of the transaction to give the consumer an attractive value proposition (see Chapter 9). This goes beyond the conception of the real estate firm as the marketer of property to the concept of the firm as transaction manager.

Like car dealers, real estate firms can grow to establish a model that maximizes volume. The mergers and acquisitions that have come seemingly daily in the real estate industry are attempts by real estate companies to do just this. The business approach of Cendant is another aspect of the power of size, if only on the cost side of the accounts. In the future, we can expect to see this trend toward mergers and acquisitions continue and grow. The real estate business of the future will be highly concentrated.

And like travel agencies, real estate professionals can concentrate on adding to the value of the services a consumer receives by becoming excellent at personalized service. It involves using expert systems (see Chapter 3) to tailor packages of services and prices exactly for each customer. This is an advantage in the market and is the reason why smaller firms will survive and thrive.

HOW DO I USE THIS RULE?

The disappearance of the middle is a major social and economic concern. But in the real estate business, it's a metaphor for the need to rethink the business model. The value in this chapter lies in pointing to new ways of thinking about the business you're in.

- The excessive reliance on the control of information is no longer a viable position to take in the marketplace.
- The real estate agent and broker need to reestablish an intermediary position that reflects the new value. Now the market will pay the guy who tells you what book you would most likely enjoy, what hotel you will be most comfortable in, how to buy the car you want at the lowest price, the best way to spend your insurance dollar . . . and what house best fits your needs.

Once you understand that the middle has disappeared and that you need to recreate the new middle, you first need to figure out what business you're in (Chapter 8). When you need to do that, you then must understand your customers (Chapter 3), so you can mine your bits (Chapter 6) and sell your own personal experience (Chapter 8).

4

Think Content

DO WHAT YOU DO

Let's take a time-out for a bit here. In this technological age, it is easy to become distracted by the bells, whistles and lights of the toys we play with every day in our business. The biggest trap may be that we think we need to be "propeller heads" to use technology effectively. This is blatantly untrue. I use electricity everyday—so do you—yet I have no idea how to wire a house, nor do I need to. By the same token I can leverage technology in my work and use it to project the power of one and lock my customers in without knowing how to program a computer or understanding how it works. I can do this because I rely on others to do it, and I concentrate on what I possess—content. My ability to create value hinges on what I know about the economy, about real estate markets and about strategic planning. In other words, my value arises from *content,* and so does yours.

FROM COMPUTER LITERATE TO
TECHNOLOGICALLY KNOWLEDGEABLE

Sometimes it seems as if information technology is some sort of black box that produces magical results. We can log onto the Internet and send e-mail to our brother in Tacoma as easily as we can phone him. We can gather information and create knowledge as easily as we can buy a newspaper. We click; it happens. Magic. And the best thing about it is that we don't even have to understand it.

In the early days of this technological revolution there was great emphasis on "computer literacy." In the Sixties, courses in Fortran were a regular part of college offerings, and we struggled to learn the grammar and vocabulary of this new language. Even later, using a computer meant having at least a nodding acquaintance with code.

That has drastically changed. Programming now is the province of a specific profession, one that has been unfortunately (and accurately) described in the cartoon, "Dilbert." For the average person, using a computer means little more than "point and click." Buying the machine is the most knowledge-filled decision in the whole process; the computer does the rest. All computers now come loaded with Internet access programs, modems to connect to the outside world, and CD-ROM players. (Power levels are a differentiating factor, but most machines are standard.)

When I want to add some new function or feature to my computer, it's a snap to buy the necessary software, plug it in and use it. When I set up my business, it took me 20 minutes to install Microsoft's Office 97. I then had at my fingertips word processing, calculating, organizing, and presentation software. In short, I was my own Wizard of Oz. Another 20 minutes gave me QuickBooks and substantially reduced the probability of the IRS throwing me into the slammer and of my accountant shooting me at tax time.

The point here is that computer literacy has become as passé for the average individual as the typewriter. The key is to know what the technology can do for you and the best way to leverage it in your business. I knew I needed the kind of software I bought, and I knew how I could employ it to make money. I was (and still am) ignorant as to how it works.

THE THREE "C's"

All this is background to a way of thinking about technology that is necessary and useful in today's real estate market. The technology revolution that has blown apart the business models of so many industries was spawned by the combination of three separate elements in varying proportions. The three elements of information technology are *computing, communication and content.*

Computing Has Had Its Day

The first of these–**computing**–is software development. Early computer users remember how important programming was. The old IBM card systems using mainframe computers were a breakthough, but they were cumbersome and slow. More importantly, they were harsh mistresses. I can recall trying to use such a system while writing my doctoral thesis. Each night I would submit a deck of cards containing my program and my data and most mornings I would find that the program had bombed. If the cards were not punched in exactly the right fields and placed in exactly the right order, the computer would not deign to honor your requests.

Even later, when the home computer was introduced, activation required the insertion of a sequence of disks. Wrong order, no service. When canned programs were introduced—mostly games, since that originally was the major use for these machines—we went to the store and spent a great deal of money to get the right programming. In the early days of computers, programming (computing) was a lucrative business.

The Internet has killed this business and made software a public good. For most programs, you can go online and get any program you want free. In fact, the elapsed time between the creation of a specific piece of software and its availability free on the Internet is rapidly approaching the half-life of a mayfly. This flows from General Rule #1: Speed Kills. Only where the software is necessary to a specific function (usually a highly sophisticated industrial application) is computing a viable business. Perhaps the only firm left that can claim to make a profit from mass market software development is Intel, and that mostly stems from basic operating software rather than applications.

Communications Is Cool—But It Ain't Easy

Three years ago, Microsoft realized that computing had run its course and shifted its focus to communications. Originally, Microsoft pursued a strategy of creating proprietary networks. Increasingly, however, these systems were surpassed by similar applications transmitted over the Internet. Microsoft shifted to an Internet strategy, in effect making a 180-degree turn, and began transmitting its software to users over the Internet through the Microsoft Network (MSN).

The second element of information technology—**communications**—deals with the systems over which information and knowledge are transmitted. The most common of these networks is the telephone system, with television and radio close behind. Each of these allows individuals to conduct business and personal affairs in real time at a distance. The phone companies and the radio and television

A • • • • • Quick and Useful Glossary, or What are You Talking About?

Hardware: Communications devices like televisions, telephones, computers and their complementary devices

Software: Computer programs designed to facilitate specific functions

Computing: The function of creating hardware and software that allows households and businesses to accomplish their ends electronically

Communications: The development and administration of a network over which information (print, sound and picture) can flow; includes the Internet, telephone, cable, television and radio

Content: Information and knowledge that can be disseminated over a network

Code: Language that governs computer functions

Programming: The creation of code combinations that instruct computers in how to execute specific functions

Network: A system of connections that serves as a channel for information and communications among communities of users.

Proprietary networks: Combinations of software and networks that serve the needs of specific users. The needs may be generic (word processing, e-mail, etc.) but the network is dedicated to an identified group of users

Geographic Information Systems: Software designed to describe a particular physical location in a variety of different dimensions simultaneously

networks are merely conduits; they facilitate the exchange of print, sound and pictures. Think of them as water mains, pipes through which something of value flows.

The march of technology over the past 150 years has brought these networks closer to the user, faster and capable of carrying increasing volumes of information. The telegraph was restricted to a single message per wire at any time. As telephone systems spread, they required more and more cabling. Now the Internet enables direct access by anyone through an ever-widening "information main" capable of carrying huge volumes of information.

Currently, networking is a mainstay of the new economy. The growing use of the Internet for information, communication and commerce means that whoever owns the channel most used by the public stands to gain a great deal of revenue. Think of the number of users of a given network as the equivalent of the Nielsen ratings. Higher ratings mean more viewers and higher advertising rates. Networks bid for the rights to broadcast the Super Bowl because of the number of eyeballs who tune in; they make the expenditure back by charging higher advertising rates. (The same holds true for "special" events like last episodes [see Chapter 2]. In fact, the only times the networks seem to show anything new, original or interesting are the February, May and November "sweeps," times when Nielsen is calculating ratings, and thus determining advertising rates.)

The communications race in information technology is to drive eyeballs to the network by setting the standards by which the public accesses information. Netscape's gamble in sending out 40 million unfinished copies of its Navigator (see Chapter 1) was an attempt to position itself as *the* network for consumers and thus exploit the profit potential of this business. Microsoft's entire strategy is based on the drive to set standards, and explains why so much is at stake in its struggle with the Department of Justice. It also explains Microsoft's strategy in entering the real estate market. It wants to set the standards by which information flows through the market and in doing so control the customer and the transaction.

Microsoft appears as a juggernaut in this field, and that may be the case. But, there are a large number of competitors, so much so that it resembles the automobile industry at the turn of the Twentieth Century. At that time, automobiles were being manufactured by about 200 auto makers—just about anyone with technical knowledge, a garage and some capital. When Ford pioneered the assembly line, the field thinned rapidly. Similarly, in communications, there are many different network providers. We just haven't yet discovered our Henry Ford.

Content Is Indispensable

The last area—**content**—is where the real value added lies. You can have the quickest, most extensive communications network in the world, but it has to contain something interesting, or no eyeballs will be there. Without content, even the best network in the world is nothing more than a telephone system—dumb wires and poles.

Think about the Web sites you've visited. How many have you revisited more than once? Why did you go back? Why didn't you go back? The odds are that the answer to these last two questions is roughly the same. You went back because the material on the Web site was refreshed, added to and updated. You didn't go back because nothing had changed.

Your judgment of the site was based on content. If the information carried by that particular channel was relevant and changing, you bought in. If you expand this to the full network, the consideration is the same. Whether it's MSN or America Online or Erol's or Delphi or any other channel to the Internet, the content that channel carries is important and will influence whether and how much you use it.

W^{hat} Goes Where: A Guide to Occupations In the Three C's

Getting a handle on the three C's is not always easy, particularly as change rips through information businesses. The Bureau of Labor Statistics classifies industries across the entire economy. If you looked at those standard classifications for media in the context of the three C's, here's what you'd find:

Computing

Computer equipment
Semiconductors and related devices
Miscellaneous electronic products
Electrical equipment and supplies
Search and navigation equipment
Computer and data processing services, software
Electrical repair shops

Communications

Communications facilities
Household A/V equipment
Telephone and telegraph equipment
Broadcasting and communications equipment
Communications, except broadcasting
Radio and TV broadcasting

Content

Newspapers
Periodicals
Books
Miscellaneous publishing
Greeting card publishing
Advertising

Photocopying, commercial art, photo finishing
Business services
Motion pictures
Video tape rental
Producers, officers and entertainers
Libraries, vocational and other schools

These categories are not completely up-to-date, since they exclude virtually all the new technology companies, but at least it's a start.
—Don Tapscott, *The Digital Economy,* (New York: McGraw-Hill, 1996), p. 329   • • • • •

The networks compete not only for users, but also for contributors. ESPN's Sportszone is a very popular site, particularly with that all-important demographic, males-without-a-life-aged-25-to-49. The ability to access that site with a single keystroke is an attraction for the public, even with the capacity to "bookmark" after a visit. Ultimately, those who can offer the most content with the easiest accessibility will be the winners in the race for profits and business.[1] The stakes are high and so are the prices the networks will pay. Those prices reflect the leverage exercised by the content providers.

---

[1] Interestingly, those companies with their own networks in other areas are attempting to enter the electronic flow by translating the content they control. For example, most newspapers and magazines now have online editions. Other companies have attempted to leverage their expertise by starting completely online magazines, and one—*Wired*—has gone the opposite route and taken an electronic concept into the print medium.

GRABBING A SERVICE NICHE

What has this meant for American business? Essentially, it has demanded that any firm in an information business— and especially real estate—rethink its core business and its delivery system. Each of these three aspects has its own value, use and applicability. However, as you might suspect, none of them is exclusive. The nature of change and the power of one has both allowed and dictated a blending of the three parts of information technology. No firm is purely a network, or purely a software company or all content. Rather, each inhabits a landscape that has features of one or more.

As the technology revolution has proceeded, old and new companies alike have attempted to position themselves in the computing–communications–content geography. Most have built upon their core business and expanded into the closest and most compatible of the other areas. Very few companies have attempted to be the all-encompassing master of the three domains.

There are, however, two examples of companies that have attempted to make the triumvirate work for them. Microsoft is the obvious example. Its roots are in computing, with the Windows 95 (presumably to be supplanted by Windows 98) operating system, the standard for all computers. As I described above, the creation of MSN moved Microsoft front-and-center into the communications area. MSN and Windows are the perfect complements in providing the user with full network accessibility and computing power.

Acquiring content has been slower, partially because a number of competitors (e.g., AOL) have been able to marshal equal content. But Microsoft has shown through Expedia and Carpoint (Will Home Advisor be next?) that it has the capacity to buy content to populate its network. In doing all this, Microsoft has placed itself (at least in the eyes of the

*C*ontent companies have been the most comfortable with staying close to home. An example here is Dow Jones, whose core business was, and is, the provision of financial information between markets and businesses. Its highest profile subsidiary, *The Wall Street Journal,* has gone online, as has its financial reporting service, but both are carried by other networks. Dow remains a content provider with some communications interests and activities.

Other content companies have moved in other directions. Disney and Paramount, for example, have migrated further down the road toward communications. Disney, by purchasing Capital Cities, has entered the broadcasting business through the conventional model. Paramount has begun its own network. General Electric, through its subsidiary NBC, has expanded its broadcast operations by initiating several cable networks.

Communications companies, likewise, have stuck close to home. AT&T has attempted to increase its software capacity and in part its content through mergers and acquisitions, particularly by adding content to its paging services.

Computing companies have attempted to expand their businesses by improving the speed and capacity of their product. The most successful of these has been Intel, which has become the standard for information processing in personal computers. Intel, in fact, has been wildly successful. There are hundreds of hardware manufacturers out there, and differentiating among them is nearly impossible for

> the public. But, the Intel "bug" on the body of the machine is all anyone needs to be assured that the computer will work. The absence of the symbol dooms the manufacturer.　• • • • •

Department of Justice) in the role of the robber barons of a century ago. This may be true, but sometimes you need a robber baron or two to push the revolution along.

The other company that has attempted to blend the three areas more or less equally is Worldcom. Once a small, regional cable TV company, Worldcom announced, through its bid to acquire the telephone giant MCI, that it would expand its network nationwide, and move into the area of content. Additionally, with its development of communications software, MCI has some aspects of a computing company.

WHAT'S THE NICHE FOR REAL ESTATE COMPANIES?

You can probably guess the answer to this question from the title of the chapter. There are two major sources of content that flow from real estate professionals and which are indispensable to communications providers. The first of these is property information. As much as the value of this information will fade away as it originates from multiple providers in many different ways (see Chapter 1), property descriptions, together with complementary information, are still the province of the real estate industry.

The second type of content is more subjective. The analysis of a piece of property goes beyond mere description. It encompasses the knowledge that the real estate practitioner possesses about the setting of the property within its full economic, political and legal context. That information is key to establishing value and increases the efficiency of the property transfer market. The communications network that offers the fullest description of the property and the corresponding market realities will appear to be superior in the eyes of the buying and selling public.

Real estate firms can position themselves as content providers and thus be important players in the new economy. Once again, the key is turning information into knowledge (see Chapter 2). That means surrounding the essentials of the property description with all complementary materials. A Geographic Information System, for example, can relate the property to employment and retail centers, transportation networks, schools, political and tax jurisdictions, and environmental and zoning restrictions. **Production of that type of content adds value for the consumer** and makes the listing a valuable market commodity. The attractiveness of listing information is attested to by Microsoft's monetary offer for MLS information.

All this means that reliance on the MLS is wise only if the MLS has the collateral descriptions that add context to the property. Increasingly, the MLS systems that do not migrate toward this end—creating knowledge by taking information and molding it into value for consumers—will find themselves abandoned by savvy firms that create that value and seek out the best buyers.

TRYING TO DO IT ALL: THE RIN EFFECT

Looking at the content companies that have ventured into the communications area, the larger firm might well ask: why can't we do alone? Why not capture the value of content by being a distributor? The simple answer to this question is that it's none of your business. That's not a snide answer, but one that's literally true: no real estate firm is in the technology business, nor should it be. Putting up a Web site does not put you into the communications business, because a site is not a network.

The poster child for this point is the REALTORS®' Information Network (RIN), a venture initiated in 1993 by the National Association of REALTORS®. RIN was designed to create the full listing context that would enable the REALTOR® to control the essential information about properties on the market. It was designed as a proprietary network that would meld the MLS with information about financing, other settlement services and a GIS.

When the project was first investigated, several communications companies were approached. It became apparent that these firms would seek ownership of the property information—a concession the Association was both unwilling and unable to give. That slanted the project in another direction, namely a wholly owned and operated subsidiary of NAR. The Association would act as content and communications company, supplying the information and creating the network for its distribution.

RIN was a failure in that it was unable to deliver both the content and communications aspects of its mission. The major problem was the inability of the Association—in effect a content provider—to create and operate a communications network. As the information business shifted from a proprietary network basis to the Internet, RIN labored on to create its own internal system. And because the RIN board did not link well to the cutting edge of technology, it missed the importance of the shift, mainly because *it was not the board's business.*

(This section does not pretend to tell the whole story of RIN, nor will I tell tales out of school. Rather, key aspects of the story are presented as a case study to indicate the pitfalls of straying too far from home when attempting to navigate the waters of the information revolution. For more on this, see Chapter 9.)

From the wreckage of RIN there emerged a new vehicle, one that has been very successful. When RIN was resuscitated, it was done through a partnership with a communications company whose expertise complemented the content strength of the NAR. One Realtor Place® was created as a password–protected site attached to NAR's public Web site, and it contained all the complementary information that would give the MLS listing context and richness. Meanwhile, the public side of the site, REALTOR.COM, loaded up MLS listings and linked to settlement service providers. By placing the entire inventory of existing homes for sale and financing information in one place, REALTOR.COM became the place for consumers to go when they entered the housing market. The site linked directly to AOL, completing the communications circle. The key point is that the lesson was learned.

The success of REALTOR.COM is rooted in the failure of RIN. The necessity for joint venturing (see Chapter 1, general rule 3) was the lesson learned from RIN. The partnership between NAR and Real Select in creating the site joined the content expertise of REALTORS® around the country with the networking knowledge of a communications company to produce an all-purpose system. That system is sufficiently robust to contend on an equal basis with the power and funding of a Microsoft. Any real estate company considering trying to do it all must study the RIN case for the lessons it can yield as well.

HOW TO USE THIS CHAPTER

Settle on the fact that you are a content expert and create a system within your company or your practice that will make you a valuable content provider to all the systems out there that want your input:

- Ensure the absolute accuracy and currency of all of your listings, your company inventory or your MLS. Assign some individual (you, a personal assistant, an employee) to watch this as his or her sole task.
- Augment your listings with a GIS that can flesh out the bare bones of the property description. This software is available for very little in a relatively easy-to-use form. If you don't want to handle it, hire someone to do it. That person can also assemble the data that makes the software work. Use the software to enhance the attractiveness of your listings to the public and thus to the communications networks.
- Evaluate the outlets for your enhanced listings and determine those most beneficial to you. Clearly, you want your efforts to pay off, but money may not be the currency here. Exposure, juxtaposition with other transaction services and consumer friendliness may give you the best use of your listings.

There is a fourth "C." Computing plus communications equals **connectivity.** Your ability to connect closely with your customer is a value creating action that will be the key to your future success. In the past, real estate professionals have done this largely through their people skills, and that was OK. As the information revolution proceeds, connectivity value is established only if you add information content to your people skills. Detailed networks are able to turn information into knowledge and will last long after individual participants do. But they need content and this is what you can provide. Doing this will drive the cost of the transaction to the consumer to zero.

Establishing yourself as a content provider will help you clarify what business you're in (Chapter 9) and let you mine your bits (Chapter 6) to sell the experience to the customer (Chapter 7).

Mine Your Bits

The industrial age, very much an age of atoms, gave us the concept of mass production, with the economies of scale that come from manufacturing with uniform and repetitious methods in any one given space and time. The information age, an age of computers, showed us the same economies of scale, but with less regard for space and time. The manufacturing of bits could happen anywhere, at any time, and, for example, move among the stock markets of New York, London and Tokyo as if they were three adjacent machine tools.

—Nicholas Negroponte, *Being Digital*, p. 163

ATOMS AND BITS

I love to read newspapers. I read five a day. It probably would be different if I had a life. Like most people, I don't read every part of every paper. Rather, I read bits and pieces and pass over others. But I get the whole paper. When I go to the newsstand, the proprietor will not let me cut the stories and features that I want to read out of the newspaper and leave the rest. (Actually, he would, but I still pay for the whole paper.)

But what if I could look at only the sections of the paper I wanted? What if I could hold on to the paper and look at stories later that I didn't want to read now, without the problem of storing the paper? What if a newspaper were delivered in the order I read it, rather than the order the publisher ordained? These changes would be extremely useful to me, and make the newspaper more valuable to me.

Yes, this is another "power of one" thing, where I get to be the master of my domain. But it's also about the differences between atoms and bits. The newspaper as it's now delivered is a collection of atoms, having a physical dimension and substance that is hard to alter quickly or easily. The delivery I desire would be through bits—electronic impulses that allow for infinite flexibility and design according to my whim.

We have become accustomed to living in a world of atoms, where things are defined by the way they appeal to our senses. They have shape, color, mass, smell and sound. Don't be alarmed—we have not abandoned that world. But in the organization and transmission of information, the technological revolution has propelled us into the world of bits—tiny electronic packages that can be combined and recombined exactly as we wish.

The importance of this shift cannot be underemphasized. The skyline of New York or Chicago is a tribute to Mr. Otis. Without the elevator as a practical mechanical application, there would be no skyscrapers. Los Angeles could have easily have been called "Fordville" since its configuration is a product of cheap and efficient automobile production. Bits will have no less an effect on information businesses than the developments of the elevator and the automobile. And real estate is an information business. In fact, most of what we've discussed in the book so far is a consequence of the shift from atoms to bits.

TRAINED BITS

Information businesses can be defined broadly, but consider the impact of the shift from atoms to bits on training and education. No degree of classroom expertise and instruction is going to produce a polished surgeon or commercial pilot. Traditionally, these skills are created through a long and expensive apprentice program. The budding surgeon assists on a variety of procedures and then is able, eventually, to lead increasingly complex operations. Pilots start with the smallest commercial aircraft as second officer and move up the ladder until they take command of the largest planes they choose to fly. Piloting the pinnacle of the commercial fleet, the 747, requires upwards of 15 years experience.

Demographics suggest that the luxury of this time span will no longer be available. The baby bust and the end of the Cold War will reduce the number of candidates for surgeon or pilot. But the volume of air travel and the number of patients requiring surgery will go down far less. Luckily, the shift from atoms to bits works well here. Simulations of flight and surgery can compress the process of training to enable would-be professionals to gain "practical" experience without the danger of harm to any living being.

Bits can be substituted for atoms to implement training processes. A surgeon can conduct any procedure at any time because information flow can take the place of the physical body and allow the surgeon to learn from mistakes without real consequence. Similarly, a flight simulator can take the place of the physical plane and train the would-be pilot much more quickly without the potential of harm to life.

The next major step in this technology will be the practical use of virtual reality, software that allows the user to enter a picture and participate fully in a particular action. Right now, virtual reality exists as a game, a sideshow attraction. In the future, it will evolve into mainstream application much as other games have been the forerunners of business and personal applications. Then the use of bits for training will achieve a far more precise efficiency than is now possible.

BITS ARE SMARTER THAN ATOMS

Today's automobiles are better than those of 10 or 15 years ago. They're also lighter. Part of the decrease in weight is in the atoms of the car: more fiberglass and plastic and less metal, largely as a reaction to fuel efficiency and emissions standards legislated by the Congress and defined by the EPA. But a great part of this change has been the substitution of bits for atoms. In the process, vehicles have become smarter.

Except for the most inexpensive cars, cruise control is a standard feature. Essentially, a package of bits is controlling the speed of your car, keeping it constant to conserve fuel and reduce the stress of highway driving. Similarly, computer chips that control fuel supply to the engine have replaced the old carburetor. In more expensive cars, bits monitor almost every system that makes the car work, and allow you to access that information to help you operate the vehicle better. The contemporary automobile has in it more computing power than existed in the world prior to 1960.

The changing nature of automobiles may be the most prominent example of how moving from atoms to bits can make machinery smarter. There are more than 30 chips for every computer in the world. The excess (since each machine only needs one) chips appear in a number of unlikely places. They're on water towers in Australia, beaming the water level to the rancher who would have to drive several hours to check it otherwise. They're on the horns of that rancher's cattle identifying their location. They're in your coffee maker so that you can wake up to a fresh pot every morning. And if you're reading this book in your hotel room while on a business trip, there's probably one in the door a few feet away.

In all of these cases, the replacement of atoms by bits has created a smarter system that delivers a higher level of service than its predecessor could. More importantly, those bits can link together. The example of Marriott's exactly-on-time breakfast service (see Chapter 3) is a story of substituting bits for atoms. Rather than have a human supervisor attempting to oversee every aspect of the breakfast preparation, Marriott uses bits to lay out the specific process that will result in the delivery of a perfectly prepared breakfast at the exact moment requested. The bits can be linked so that the toast goes down three minutes before the eggs are done and the eggs are cooked just as the bacon is ready. None of this is high–level computing; it's merely the use of linked bits to produce a mechanical process that is more precise and efficient than possible before.

BITS ARE MORE VALUABLE THAN ATOMS

Consider the biggest problem in the movie rental business. Here's the scenario (no pun intended). You go to your local Blockbuster store with plans for a quiet Friday night at home, losing the tensions of the work week with an ordered-in pizza and "Scream 2." When you get there, you discover that your movie choice is unavailable. Now, your image of Blockbuster and brand loyalty is dented, if not broken. How can Blockbuster assure that when you walk in, it will have what you seek? It could stock as many copies of "Scream 2" as it could possibly rent, but this is an inventory policy that cuts deeply into profits.

An alternative is to substitute bits for atoms. The movie can be broken down into digital form and the bits relayed from a central point via satellite to any Blockbuster store and reassembled in minutes. The result is that Blockbuster can guarantee that any movie it has is always available in any location. The use of bits (the digital form of the film) has replaced atoms (the physical cassette) and in the process,

Blockbuster has enhanced its brand (see Chapter 7) and locked in its customer (see Chapter 3).

JAVA, APPLETS AND BILL GATES

Probably one of the most important applications of bits has come in the form of Java (the programming language, not the Indonesian island). Java allows for the transmission of packages of bits electronically, allowing the user to access exactly what he needs exactly when he needs it. It is the equivalent of the just-in-time inventory system that has changed the parameters of the automobile industry.

Microsoft uses Java to "rent" software. Let's say that you are creating settlement documents using Microsoft Word as your word processing software. The client you are dealing with is using Lotus WordPerfect. You can send translation software with your document so that it can be read in the other system. When the translation has been accomplished, the software disappears. You pay a few cents per use, but it saves both of you from jumping through hoops at a much greater cost.

By the way, those pennies add up. Go back to the newspaper example that opened this chapter. Suppose I paid for my paper on the basis of what I "read" at the rate of a penny a story. Suppose further that the writer of the story received half a cent. A front page story in the *Washington Post* would net the writer about $1500. I think he'd like that deal. Pennies and bits add up.

WHAT'S IN IT FOR ME?

By now you're thinking: this is all very nice, and yet another academic treatise on the new technologies, but how can I use it? Think about Microsoft and about our reporter friend above. They can command a fee because they possess knowledge that other people want. I need the Microsoft programming to do my business; the reading public wants to know about the latest developments in Asia and what they mean. So we pay.

There are enormous numbers of people who have a need to know about real estate. Historically, REALTORS® have gathered tons of data. The MLS systems record sales statistics, including property and buyer and seller information. More detailed descriptions of households, including income, home values, etc., exist in the files of the real estate office. All this information is valuable both as a product by itself and as a device to bind the client closer to you.

Marketing Property Information

Think about property information. We can identify a raft of users who would love to know specifics about parcels of property.

- *State and local governments* derive a significant portion of their tax revenues from real estate. Their ability to know the particulars (including ownership) of every piece of property in their jurisdictions would enhance their revenue generating power. Specific property information would also help guide their economic development efforts by displaying the configuration of properties in different areas.
- *Financial institutions* interested in evaluating their current loan portfolios and assessing areas of potential lending can use specific and detailed property information.
- *Market research companies* involved in selection for retail, industrial, hospitality and development sites would value complete and comprehensive property descriptions.

- *Settlement service providers* absolutely need complete information for assessments, title searches and loan underwriting.
- *Casualty insurers* could assign risk more accurately with histories of neighborhoods and individual properties.
- *Attorneys* involved in civil suits can better evaluate liability with full property description.
- *Private investigators* looking for hidden or lost property need accurate up-to-date records to identify ownership.

All of these are potential clients for the packages of information bits that make up the full description of the property. Your records, your firm's records and the MLS data make up as full a set of property information as exists anywhere. When arranged and analyzed, they are a valuable market product that can be "rented" to any of the businesses above and can create an attractive sideline for the real estate practitioner or firm, or the MLS.

Marketing People

The second set of information that you possess that contains value is the socioeconomic profiles of your clients and customers. No one knows more about the personal affairs of the individual than does her banker or her REALTOR®. Both ask and receive personal and financial information as complete as the individual can supply.

Even though they have this information, neither banks nor real estate firms use it as a marketable database. There are hundreds of firms who would pay a great deal of money for the information now in the files of the average real estate firm. Yes, it does sound crass to place the trust of your clients on the trading block, but it's done on a regular basis throughout the economy. When those annoying telemarketers call you at dinnertime, when those catalogues stuff your mailbox, and when you receive eight offers a week for new credit cards, it's because someone sold your name and information from some mailing list.

THE INFOMEDIARY

Just about the only people who don't make money off consumer information are the consumers themselves. The average guy who fills out an application of any sort, or subscribes to a magazine, or even just gets a driver's license, is immediately the target of marketing pitches from any number of firms. These pitchmen paid real money for the leads. If you're a member of NAR, that might have been one of the sources, since NAR occasionally rents its membership list.

A relational database, one that can link some aspects of information about an individual into other, broader sets of information, creates knowledge for a marketer and thus has value. The concept of an infomediary attempts to address this for the benefit of the consumer. An infomediary assembles and sorts consumer information, links it to other relational databases and sells the product to marketing firms. The proceeds are then forwarded to the owners of the information, the consumers.

Real estate professionals hold a great deal of consumer information and may be reluctant to create a business selling their customers' lives into the marketplace. The alternative may be to become the infomediary representing the consumer. After all, brokerage is brokerage, whether it's property or information.

Privacy and the Net

In May 1998 American Express announced a strategic partnership with a database marketing company designed to sell detailed data about the purchases of American Express customers. With the data resources of the partner firm (information on 175 million individuals), American Express would offer its member merchants information on consumers who were not American Express cardholders. The first part of the partnership was aimed at increasing revenue to both firms, while the second would develop for American Express a competitive edge against Visa. Both sides would provide different pieces for a data profile that would enable merchants to target their highest potential customers.

But all this was not to be. Privacy advocates raised such strong objections that American Express backed off of its plan. A privacy bill was even introduced in Congress. The American Express retreat follows the example of companies like America Online, Pacific Bell and CVS, who also withdrew plans for data mining. The tension between the potential profitability of data mining and the right to privacy by individuals is an issue that has been given sharp focus by the proliferation of the Web. There is no uniform solution available, nor is there likely to be in the future. If you choose to venture into the data mining business, be aware that you will have to address privacy issues if you are to be successful.

DOING FOR YOURSELF

Mining your bits is useful not only to create ancillary business products to enhance your income; it is also useful in attracting listings and helping buyers achieve their ends. Consider the power of a listing presentation that uses relational databases to pinpoint the location of the most probable buyers. Using bits, you can put together a package that shows the potential seller the sales history for similar homes and describes completely the demographics of the buyers. Added to that are the behavioral patterns of those potential buyers and from these the most effective ways to reach them. You are creating for that seller a listing and marketing program that will absolutely reduce the time on the market for that home.

On the buyer side, having a full property description for all the homes the buyer wishes to see makes you a more valuable resource than your competitors. Adverse local conditions, commuting patterns, job locations and other questions are handled quickly and easily. With a Geographic Information System (GIS), you can display those factors graphically and even give the customer a printed map with the requested information. In short, mining your bits will add directly to your bottom line in your main business line.

HEIGH-HO, HEIGH-HO . . .

The process by which you can create this business is called *data mining*. It is essentially the process of taking existing information on people and properties and combining them with other databases to create full information pictures. These can then be related to other databases to create even richer profiles. For example, using the names and addresses in your files, you can link through these to consumer behavior databases to create investment and con-sumption profiles that are of interest to marketing firms.

Think about the Publix example in Chapter 3. Publix gathers personal information on its customers and then adds to that the specific items individuals purchase. By linking the customer address to census tract data, Publix can add income and home value information to the file. Using the customer's Social Security number allows for even more information to be imported from other sources. Now Publix can say that the John Jones household has an annual income of about $100,000, lives in a $350,000 house and uses a certain list of items. Its members always vote, own two and a half cars with total value of $50,000, read two newspapers a day, watch three hours of television and subscribe to four magazines. Oh, and we can be more spe-cific about the TV shows, the newspapers and the maga-zines, if you wish.

Having that information in hand is extremely important to anyone who wants to sell the Jones family anything. It enables the marketing effort to be targeted, efficient and low-cost. Publix gets a big bang out of its data mining by sending just the most useable coupons to its customers, locking in their loyalty.

UNDER ALL IS THE LAND

Property information, like people information, can be combined into packages of bits that have value in the market. Each piece of property has a story to tell and that story has many different layers. From the ground up, a given parcel of land can be described in different aspects:

- *Environmental data* will describe the particular character of the land itself. From the viewpoint of the property transaction, for example, it's valuable to know the property's position relative to 50 and 100 year floodplain locations.

- *Parcel data* will list ownership, valuation, sales history and size.
- *Street level data* can include classification (arterial, etc.), the number of traffic lanes and traffic volumes.
- *Zoning data* will provide the basic status plus any variances or non-performing uses.
- *Permit data* includes building permit value, cost of construction, and the certificate of occupancy.
- *Structural data* describes building type, building height and square footage.

All these can be plotted out using Geographic Information Systems, and displayed together to give a full picture of the property. When included with adjacent parcels, the picture can be blown up to the level of whatever jurisdiction is of interest.

DATA MINING FOR RESIDENTIAL SETTLEMENT

There is a body of information that can be developed through data mining to be used in the settlement process. In the area of mortgage services and insurance, such a list would include:

- Appraisal (data and/or automated system output) and 1003 information
- Ownership, lien, assessment and tax information for both origination and home equity lending
- Loan to value ratios and portfolio analysis for purchasing first and home equity mortgages
- Lending activity reports, market share reports, mortgage deed recordings, tax reports and sales management reports
- Environmental due diligence

None of these are readily available to the real estate professional. But with the property and household information as a base, the practitioner can partner with a data service to create the full picture needed by lenders and insurers.

WHERE DO I START?

Your goal here is to create databases that contain knowledge about properties and households that will give you an edge in obtaining listings and servicing buyers, and are attractive to other users.

The initiating point of any data mining operation in real estate is the property information itself. Your own listing data, your company's records and the MLS data will describe properties that are currently on the market or have recently sold. The key to building a knowledge base of property data is to concentrate on the legal description of the property. All other information that will be combined with the basic property identification is tagged by this legal description. Especially important is census tract information. This will enable you to link into environmental and zoning information. (Generally, data about the number and type of room and their size has little value here; overall square footage is important.)

The legal description of the property will enable linkage with zoning, title and sales history data. This last piece is important as it will help establish the rate of appreciation in particular neighborhoods. Legal description will also enable the property to be placed within the context of employment and transportation patterns. You will be able to construct a full picture and history of individual pieces of property.

The second vein in your data mine is information about your clients and customers. Every real estate practitioner requests that customers fill out a detailed financial form as the first step in finding a home to buy. The form is less than official; it's designed to narrow the price range for the home search and thus save time. If the real estate professional helps the customer apply for a mortgage (an increasingly frequent occurrence), more detail, in verifiable form, becomes available. This information is generally ignored after the customer has either purchased a house or gone on to another practitioner.

Yet, the data are invaluable. Like banks, real estate offices contain in their files volumes of information that can illustrate the linkages between economic and demographic characteristics. Dredge out those files. They can be sorted, aggregated and analyzed to present specific profiles to be used in marketing. You can use the profiles to create listing presentations as I've described above. Other marketing operations will buy the information, link it to other databases and target their products to specific groups. Yet others will be interested in the specific names and addresses to feed the telemarketing mill.

I Can't Do This Alone

Yes, you're right, you can't do it alone. Nor should you (see Chapter 9). Your business is real estate, marketing homes and, more broadly, creating a channel for the delivery of consumer information and knowledge services. Here is a place to use the third general rule (strategic partnering).

To create a truly effective data mining operation, you need not just the mine (your records, the MLS data and public records) but a *miner.* The miner may come in the form of a firm specifically set up to do the mining (there are now some in operation, even in real estate) that can be engaged to set up a process through which your information can be combined with other databases to transform information into knowledge. It can be the MLS that has created a data mining business to offset the incursion of the Internet on its business. And it can even be the graduate student or professor at the local university who can implement the statistical processes that will sort your information and use the Internet to link it to other databases.

The key here is to explain carefully to the "miner" your desired end result and the information that you have in your files. The process will be long and laborious, mainly because your information will be in hard copy form and will have to be converted to electronic bits. But with the right partner, it will be worth the effort.

The second half of this process is to explore outlets for your information. Using your bits to create excellent listing presentations has the obvious customer—you. But the other bits will go to other areas. While your miner is digging away, you might want to be investigating the potential customer base for your new products.

HOW DO I USE THIS CHAPTER?

Data mining is a relatively new area of commerce—one spawned by the revolution in information technology. Mining your bits will make you a better real estate professional as well as open up potential business lines outside real estate. You are in possession of a valuable resource in the information you have on properties and individuals. But, like all resources, only by identifying a use can you make it valuable.

- Identify the specific pieces of information that you can access and which may be valuable in the marketplace. Start with your own files and the files of your firm, then look to the MLS and any public records you can obtain.

- Consult with a database specialist who can tell you the other databases publicly available that will link with and enhance the information you have.
- Partner with a data "miner" who can set up the software you need to organize your bits and reform them into valuable knowledge
- Investigate potential outlets for your bits, including your own listing presentations

Creating outstanding listing presentations can be done through the power of one (Chapter 2) and help lock your customers in (Chapter 3). It will also help clarify what business you're in (Chapter 9) and can offset the vanishing middle (Chapter 4).

Sell the Experience, Not the Product

> The first new (or newly identified) offering occurs when a company intentionally uses goods as *props* and services as the *stage* for *engaging* the customer in such a way that it creates a *memorable event*. Its economic offering is no longer the goods and services themselves, but the ***experiences*** they create.[1]
>
> –James H. Gilmore and B. Joseph Pine II, "Beyond Goods and Services," *Strategy and Leadership*, May/June 1997, p. 13

WHEN YOU WISH UPON A STAR

Probably no public company has had as universal an impact on the American household as Disney. With a core purpose–"to make people happy"–it has migrated from an animation shop to a feature production studio to a theme park developer to an international media conglomerate to a land and housing developer. At each stage it has touched the American public with an image of wholesome fun. Yet, what really does Disney do?

The vast majority of American families have crossed the threshold of either Disneyland in California or Walt Disney World in Florida. When you go to a Disney theme park, you don't get rides that are appreciably different from those at Coney Island in New York, or King's Island in Cleveland or any of dozens of other parks throughout the United States.

---

[1] Reprinted with permission from Strategic Leadership Forum.

Rather, you enter (their words, not mine) a "Magic Kingdom." You are never a "customer," but a "guest." The Disney "cast members" (not "employees" or "associates") never stop reminding you of that. And all the "cast members," from the guy in the Mickey Mouse suit to the maid who makes up your hotel room, do all in their power to immerse you fully in the wonderful world of Disney. From the time you enter the grounds and park your car in the Goofy lot to the time you drive out you have purchased an *experience*.

McDonald's is a more prosaic example of the creation of an experience. Blindfold me and take me to any McDonald's store in the U.S. When you remove the blindfold, I will be able to tell you where I am. Every sensory cue—colors, smells, sights—has been replicated in every store. I will see a great deal of red and yellow. The furniture (and some would say the food) is molded plastic, and there are a goodly number of young people working behind a counter. The experience has been molded to create a comfort zone which allows clear images to come to mind when "somebody says McDonald's." It's not the food that draws customers—McDonald's fried burgers are generally considered to be inferior to Burger King's grilled meat. People come because they know what to expect and they will get it. I can remember after a long day and a harrowing drive to a place I had never been before stumbling into a McDonald's by the side of the road and bolting down a burger and fries just for the comfort it offered, in both taste and surroundings.

There are many other examples. Starbucks is as much an ambiance as a coffee shop; when you walk in you know you'll see far too many Gen Xers behind the counter, you'll be addressed in a pseudo-foreign tongue (grande? venti?) and you'll wait a long time to be served. Nordstrom is all wood and personal shoppers and the piano player, and, incidentally, clothing.

ECONOMIC EVOLUTION

The emphasis on experience instead of product is another step in the general economic evolution we have undergone. Initially, economies were based on extraction—farming and mining—and the social structure was built accordingly. People lived on farms or in small towns and commerce was limited. The industrial revolution changed the economic base from extraction to fabrication. Now the major economic activity was the creation of "products." Once more social organization followed economics, and large cities became the focus.

Increasingly, products became commodities—that is, the specific differentiation between brands disappeared and the lowest price was the deciding factor for the purchaser. At that point, manufacturing gave way to services as the driving sector of the economy. This shift coincided with the beginning of the technological revolution. There is a paradox here. Information technology has speeded up change in all aspects of the economy and society. In doing so, it has broken down the ability of a manufacturer to set his product off from all others. This "commoditization" of goods has been accelerated by the purchase of well-known labels by conglomerates and the subsequent merchandising of these labels through the ubiquitous "outlet" malls that clog the highways. This tactic has managed to reduce the value of what previously had been exclusive nametags. Yet, in times of rapid change, brands are a source of comfort for consumers who will be attracted to them.

In the new economy, even service has given way to something else. Product has melded with delivery system to create experience. The parts are inseparable. If you think about how Disney and McDonald's and Starbucks are selling themselves, if you envision all the ads for these and other companies, the impression they seek to create is that of a total experience. They have gone beyond simply product or service to something more, something that blends the two.

BRANDING

All this has changed the very nature of brand names. The old concept of branding was that a product could be counted on for a specific level of quality because of its label. Name brands in food could be safely assumed to be of higher quality than store brands. Cadillacs were "better" than Oldsmobiles. To a great extent that still holds true. But product quality has compressed. Now, most supermarkets offer high quality foods under their own label. Automobiles are very close to being the same regardless of the price range.

In short, goods have become commodities, where price is the main decision factor. This is in part the reason why the middle has vanished (see Chapter 4) in retailing. The rise of the category-buster chains like Wal-Mart has followed on the heels of brand compression in products.

Yet, there are clearly still brands. Nordstrom and Neiman-Marcus still compete with Wal-Mart. The survival of brands has occurred not so much because of the product offered, but rather because of the experience provided. We remember the interaction with the establishment more than we remember the quality of the product we purchased. If the "Pirates of the Caribbean" has long lines on a 100-degree day in Orlando, our perception of Disney is far less charitable than it might be. Some brands are so valuable that they can become whole businesses. Sara Lee, for example, has gotten out of the manufacturing business altogether and now just manages its brands (see Chapter 9).

For any business, the key to creating a brand is the delivery of a consistently superlative experience to every customer. That experience should also be the same experience and it should match as nearly as possible the customer's expectations about his interaction with the company. That requires the development and implementation of a system that will not vary from location to location or from time period to time period.

The true brands have done this. McDonald's is a case in point. There is no variation in the taste of McDonald's food from one day to the next or from one corner of the country to another. The music you hear in the Nordstrom in Seattle sets the same mood as the music you hear in McLean, Virginia. And you wait the same time for your coffee in any Starbucks in the country. This has to happen because perception of brand excellence based on experience unfolds over a period of time. If the system cannot be sustained and be consistent across the entire business, it will fail, and no brand identity will have been established.

Brands become increasingly important in times of rapid change. They are a substitute for information in the market. If I know nothing about computers (as is the case with most of us) I can look for the Intel logo on the body of the machine to assure me that I'm making a credible purchase. When we are most unsure, the brand becomes more valuable. For most companies, the development of a brand is the single most valuable activity it can undertake.

THERE ARE NO EXPERIENCES ON THE INTERNET

Creating a brand in the new economy may seem very difficult, since most activity will be technologically connected. Because there is no physical presence and because it engages only the sense of sight and hearing, there are no "experiences" on the Internet. Because of this, there can be no brands on the Internet, or, more broadly, no company can establish a brand through the Internet.

But what about Amazon.com? Isn't that a brand? While it has some characteristics of a brand, it's more of an efficient variation on a particular product. Most customers use physical bookstores to get the touch and feel of a book and even take some time to read from it. Amazon then becomes the convenient, discount-priced delivery system. It has the potential to become a brand the way that Federal Express, for example, is a brand. But it has not yet created that consistency of experience that is required for brand status.

Technology, however, can play a key role in brand development. The consistent experience that is required can best be accomplished using replicable systems, and these are most efficiently done using technology. The consistency of McDonald's fries is achieved because the cooking process is computerized. No fry is cooked any differently from any other anywhere because the human element is removed and the cooking process is under the control of a machine.

Similarly, the part of Disney World that you can't see is more fascinating than the part you can. Behind the scenes (this is an experience, you know) are miles of tunnels that connect parts of the park and contain tons of machinery. This allows for the rapid removal of dirt, debris and garbage which otherwise would mar the experience of the Magic Kingdom. In the exhibits themselves, computers determine the nature of the experience the guest receives. In the Hall of Presidents, Abe Lincoln can't forget his lines or cough at the wrong time, because that would change the experience, so computers do the work and the planning.

So the creation of a consistent experience which is the key to achieving a brand identity is facilitated by the use of technology. The effect here is kind of a reverse Wizard of Oz. Now the machinery and the thunder and lightning is *behind* the curtain. In front is the folksy, service-oriented wizard.

THERE ARE NO BRANDS IN REAL ESTATE

The real estate business is only slowly coming to this realization. We have nameplates in the real estate industry, but no brands. The franchises—Coldwell Banker, Century 21, ERA, BH&G, Re/Max, etc.—are recognizable to the public pretty much nationally. Within a given market area, we can identify Long & Foster or Weichert or Realty One or Windermere. But there are no brands.

There are no real estate firms in this country where the consumer receives the same experience (in the sense of Disney or Starbucks or Nordstrom) each time he or she enters an office of that firm. No two offices produce the same experience; in fact, no single office can promise the same experience from day to day. Try it yourself. Go to a real estate office on two consecutive days and see if you get the same experience. Compare notes with your colleagues around the country. Can they provide counter examples?

The argument at this point is that real estate is such an individualized process that each customer has to be treated individually. This is true, but I may choose a different route through Disney World than you, but we would both be clear that we were in the same park. Too often, individual service is an excuse for the lack of a consistent system of dealing with customers.

Yet, in a world of change and chaos, brands that offer a steady and reliable experience are sought out and used by consumers. The closest thing to brands in the real estate industry are the top producing agents, and even there the absolute replication of experience is not present.

There are two reasons for the lack of branding in real estate. The first is the *independent contractor status* of most agents. In theory, all sales licensees are independent contractors with only a temporary relationship with a particular firm. Their services are engaged on a particular compensation arrangement and that's pretty much the end of the firm's control. The licensee is responsible for his own hours, expenses, and work activities. The firm may set some standards, and the National Association of REALTORS® provides ethical guidelines, but that's about it.

But the independent contractor status, while valid for tax purposes, is not simon-pure. The regulatory bodies of each state require that all sales licensees "hang" their license in a broker's office. Firms routinely refer to "their" sales associates and measure size by the number of licenses they hold. Additionally, the name of the brokerage must be more prominent than that of the licensee in all public representations. So there is a bit of an employee relationship in the industry. The sales associates are certainly the face of the company to the public.

Sales associates have very different approaches to the client, and they exemplify different levels of competence and experience. All have probably been trained in the routine that the company employs in obtaining listings, working leads and servicing buyers. The degree to which these are followed will, of course, vary from associate to associate. In a way, the broker is in much the same position as a high school or college football or basketball coach, whose fame, reputation and income are all in the hands of some hormonally challenged 18–year–olds. Sales associates may not be that flighty, but you get the point.

The second reason for the lack of branding in real estate is related to the first. Brokers cannot be sure of their workforce because of the independent contractor status. At any time, the majority of his sales associates (there's that phrase again! If they're independent, how can they belong to a particular firm?) can just walk to another firm with a better offer. He can entice them to stay by offering better compensation or making their jobs easier by office procedures or technology. But *the focus of the broker is always on the agents, not the customer.* (The analogy would be if Disney operated Disney World for the ease and convenience of the cast members and not the guests.)

So the broker has not invested in the systems that would ease the transaction for the customer. Even for those brokers who have mortgage and title companies, relocation companies or other ancillary businesses, there are no transaction manager systems that would provide the consistency of experience that is identified with a brand. It's not worth the effort as long as a shifting group of associates is responsible for implementation of the system.

Top producers have achieved a kind of branding. In most cases, they work with one or more personal assistants who execute an ordered series of work tasks that feed into the transaction. While seldom automated, these tasks constitute a "system" that can be applied to each and every customer. And while the agent gives each customer personalized attention and service, every customer goes through the same sequence of paperwork administered by the assistants. It is this attention to detail, this transaction "experience" that brings customers back and provides referrals to their relatives and friends.

CAN THERE BE BRANDS IN REAL ESTATE?

Branding is difficult in real estate under the current culture. Right now, the agent handles virtually all aspects of the transaction under the gateway model. The consumer has access to the full services of the settlement process only after he has entered the door the real estate professional opens. Much of this work is tedious, repetitive, and far too mundane to fetch the kind of prices that real estate licensees charge. When you buy a new car, the salesman shows you the car and negotiates a price. That done, you are turned over to a customer service representative who handles all the paperwork with you. The salesman is off to the next customer.

In the real estate business, all the routine paperwork is handled under the supervision of the licensee, under the guise of full service. There are a lot of reasons to use a real estate professional in a real estate transaction; carrying papers to the mortgage lender is not one of them. Yet, most licensees quote a single price, and don't differentiate among the professional and clerical tasks they will perform for that compensation.

As technology turns the gateway model into a jigsaw puzzle that anyone can put together, branding in real estate becomes a more realistic goal. With modern information technology, the real estate transaction can be broken down into component parts, each of which can be assigned to its most appropriate executioner. Home search or listing design, mortgage application, title search, appraisal, home inspection and settlement appointments can be handled by a transaction manager who need not have a real estate license. Showing homes, negotiating a contract and counseling buyers and sellers is reserved for the real estate professional.

BRANDING AT THE AGENT LEVEL

This model in some ways resembles the process used by the top agents in the real estate industry. Because of the independent contractor shield, they have been able to assemble "firms–within–firms," in effect building a system that assigns to individuals specialized tasks that comprise the real estate transactions. Without the burden of the independent contractor status, top producers can hire employees to make the model work. They create their own individual brands.

It is entirely possible that any agent can establish this kind of brand identity. Clearly, the more transactions you do, the easier it becomes to use a system, both logistically and financially. And the more consistent and satisfying "experiences" you provide for your customers, the stronger your brand becomes. At the very least, you can establish a routine, a system, that relies as much as possible on the Internet to present a clear identity to the public.

BRANDING AT THE FIRM LEVEL

This is a lot more feasible, if no less easy. To create a brand, the broker needs to take control over the majority of the transaction. This allows salaried clerical employees (let's call them customer service representatives–CSRs) to execute the routine functions of the transaction and allow the independent contractor to handle the expert portions of the deal. For the most part, the CSRs should be technologically trained and know their way around the Internet. They should also be acquainted with the definitions of appraisal, title and inspection and be able to speak effectively with those who provide these services. Finally, they ought to be able to guide a customer through the process of home search on the Internet and mortgage choice and application. In other words, they are part clerks and part counselors.

THE BRANDED FIRM

Your face to the world is controlled and consistent. All your offices have the same exterior look, with color scheme, logo, sign placement, doors and windows the same for each of your locations. When the customer enters the office, she is greeted by a customer service representative and ushered

*T*he systems handled by the CSR should include:

Home search: Using the Internet, the CSR should be able to help potential buyers narrow down their home choices.

Mortgage choice and application: The CSR should be able to explain the various features of different mortgage products available from a variety of lenders and then guide the customer through the application process.

Title search: The CSR should be able to use the Internet or public records to search the title on the houses under consideration for purchase. Soon, this will be done over the Internet by direct connection to public records. In those 10 percent of the cases where title is cloudy, the services of a professional title company will be necessary.

Appraisal: The CSR will arrange for and handle the results of the appraisal of the property. Again, something that will eventually be done in the office by the CSR using the Internet. The URL (web address) appraisal.com is already reserved.

E-mail: The CSR will arrange for all the necessary inspections and schedule the settlement date using e-mail.

Document exchange: The CSR will oversee the transfer of all necessary documents to all relevant parties.

The rest of the process—listing presentation, contract negotiation and filing, and counseling—are the responsibility of the licensed agent.

into a comfortable room with full technological connections, including Internet hookup.

Each CSR goes through the same orientation process for the consumer: personal information, a short questionnaire on expectations and an inquiry as to whether the customer is already working with a particular agent. The CSR then explains the homebuying transaction and the steps the consumer will go through, the amount of time each should take and who will be working with them at each stage and the cost. The CSR then lays out the expectations of the firm toward the customer: information to be provided, appointments to be kept, etc.

That done, the CSR and the customer access the Internet and proceed to search REALTOR.COM for available inventory, eventually narrowing down the search to three or four possibilities. The CSR then explains mortgage options to the customer and guides the customer through a mortgage application, videoconferencing with the loan officer if necessary.

At this point, the CSR turns the customer over to a licensee who will show the chosen properties. While this is happening, the CSR will search title and seek appraisals on each of the chosen properties, keeping in telephone contact with the licensee should any other homes be added to the search. When the customer and the licensee return, contract in hand, the CSR will arrange for the rest of the settlement process by e-mailing inspectors, attorneys and any other necessary entities.

During the time between the contract and the settlement (probably shortened by the application of your system and the work of the CSR), the customer service representative will handle all documents, assuring they reach the right hands at the right time. He will also maintain contact with the customer to ensure that all questions are answered and that the customer has full knowledge of each step of the transaction.

From beginning to end, your name is prominent to the customer as the brand creating this experience. You have provided a smooth and satisfying experience for the customer and the same experience for every customer. To ensure that this happens the same way all the time, you follow each transaction with a quality control interview and you meet with all your CSRs monthly to detect any weaknesses in the system.

HOW DO I GET THERE FROM HERE?

Creation of a brand is not easy. To begin with, it requires that you exercise more control and direction over the transaction. For agents, this is relatively easy. They can use REALTOR.COM to display property inventory and can hook into various computerized loan origination systems to provide their customers with the widest range of options for financing the home purchase. They can hire assistants and provide them with forms and procedures that are consistent across customers and clients. But even with this, the degree of branding they can accomplish is limited.

Brokers have the ability to achieve full branding, but are hampered in creating a consistent experience. Some larger firms have begun the process through the use of 800 numbers, hotlines that attract the public directly to their services, and referral business. If the call is a seller, they can assign the listing to an in-house licensee over whom they exercise direct quality control; for a referral, they assign the customer similarly to an in–house agent. The broker can process these listings through an internal system that provides the same route for all buyers and sellers.

The problem comes when the broker attempts to push the system to all his offices. Creating the consistent experience for all buyers and sellers means far more broker control over what happens in each office. Décor and technology are the easy parts. Convincing agents to defer to a CSR who is in effect the transaction manager is difficult in current practice. It probably can't be done with the best agents. On the other hand, average agents may find that the implementation of the system helps them organize themselves better and concentrate on counseling the customer.

At the very least, the broker needs to implement a full transactions system that is as automated as possible. Doing so will save the customer time and stress and move to the point where all transactions look alike. In the jigsaw puzzle model, any number of people can serve as the manager that puts the transaction together. You have an advantage now because the public is used to coming to the real estate firm first. Developing a consistent experience for the consumer will help you keep that edge.

HOW CAN I USE THIS CHAPTER?

Increasingly, products, or even services, are not enough for success in the market. The most successful firms offer the consumer a melding of product and service into an experience delivered over a period of time. Real estate professionals need to create that delivery of experience to maintain their edge in the real estate market.

As you absorb this chapter, consider the following steps:

- Review your business processes. How consistent is the experience of consumers who deal with you and your firm?
- Find out where the experience can be made more consistent immediately. It can be a simple as having each customer greeted at each of your offices by people with the same training and following the same script.

- Can you homogenize the look of your offices, so it's immediately apparent to the consumer where he is?
- Do you have a system in place that takes consumers from the beginning to the end of the transaction in the same way? Is that route the fastest and most efficient you can provide?
- Can you move within your firm to a CSR type approach and let your licensees concentrate on providing expert assistance to customers and clients?

Coming as close to creating a brand as possible is important in today's market. Consumers, buffeted by change, are looking for the haven of brands they can trust. With the jigsaw puzzle model, there are a lot of folks out there looking to be the real estate brand.

By creating an experience for the customer, you lock him in for life (Chapter 3), and you clarify the business you're in (Chapter 9). In addition, you can capture the new middle (Chapter 4).

Feed the OODA Loop

VERIFYING YOU

Verifone is a company you've probably never heard of, but with which you have contact at least once a week. When you make a purchase using a credit card, the validity of that card is verified, usually electronically. Verifone creates the software that accomplishes the verification.

It's a company that stays very close to its market. Its global offices are named after the airports they are near, rather than the cities in which they are located. The reason for this is that 50 percent of Verifone's staff is in the field 80 percent of the time, sensing the needs of customers. To ensure that the information thus gathered is injected into the company's processes, all communication is accomplished by e-mail. (All employees, up to and including the chairman, are accessible by e-mail.) To ensure that the information is interpreted properly, all company records are available to every staff member.

Whenever a new product is being created, usually in response to an observation made by the staff in the field, it is worked on around the clock. Suppose that product development is initiated in San Francisco. When it's time to go home, the development process is transferred to Tokyo, which accordingly transfers it to Europe, then to New York and then back to San Francisco, chasing the sun and minimizing development time.

This is possible because Verifone is a worldwide company, but also because its processes and culture are set up to sense market opportunities and seize upon them quickly. The field staff are constantly in touch with customers; the internal communications system is quick and lean; each staff member knows everything about the workings of the company; development continues around the clock and around the globe. This method of doing business has allowed Verifone to stay at the top of its business.

THE OODA LOOP

In a world where microscopic edges often yield big profits and then disappear rapidly (see the last general rule in Chapter 1), the ability to recognize those edges and act on them is an enormous competency. It is also an essential one.

Verifone exemplifies the OODA loop, whose initials stand for "observe, orient, decide and act" (see Figure 8.1). The placement of so many staff close to the customers allows the company to *observe* where the market is heading and what its customers want and need. The freedom of information throughout the company allows the staff to *orient* the company toward the importance of the information to the goals of the organization. E-mail communication facilitates the process of *deciding* how to react to the information. Continuous global operations let the company *act* in a timely and effective manner.

FIGURE 8.1 The OODA Loop

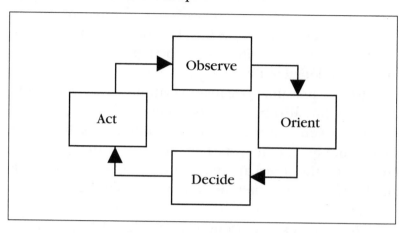

Following the OODA loop is absolutely essential to anyone in this world of constant and accelerating change. It is rooted in trend spotting, but goes far beyond that. Trend spotting without any backup is merely the notation of fads. For example, the Spice Girls are a fad. With analysis, though, they can be seen as a symbol of the assertiveness of young women in creating and maintaining their own lifestyles.

These lifestyles result in independent consumption decisions that create marketing opportunities in a whole range of industries from clothing to publishing to entertainment to education. With a system that works the full OODA loop, it is possible to stay on top of where your markets are going and to get there before the customers arrive, positioning yourself as the key supplier of their needs and wants.

But using the OODA loop also goes beyond understanding the market. It entails being ready to act as soon as you understand what is happening and what it means for your business. That requires an operation that can digest and use information immediately. Verifone has the advantage of being worldwide in operation, but that's not necessary. It takes the resources, will and organization to make real what you know will be profitable.

REAL ESTATE AND THE OODA LOOP

In real estate, the OODA loop has been remarkable by its absence. The business as it has been run does not lend itself to the integrated use of information about the future. The nature of the business has required concentration on the next listing, the next sale, the next closing. The ability to look six or twelve months into the future has never been a well-developed characteristic of the industry. This is not a criticism. Under the old gateway model, this was an absolutely appropriate approach to the market.

More importantly, it is often very difficult to understand the significance of market developments even if you know what they are. A case in point from outside of real estate is our last "crisis" with Iraq. The newspapers and the electronic media devoted endless hours to the question of whether we would be going to war with a fourth-rate power that stood no chance of doing any major harm to the United States. In the same time period, the administration and the Congress were entering negotiations about the standards that would be used to encode sensitive data on the Internet. This latter issue was of infinitely higher importance to the American people than was Iraq, yet very little media attention was devoted to it.

This is also the case with real estate. The baby–boom generation has been around for over 50 years, and for the last two decades we have been admitting immigrants to the U.S. in near record numbers. Yet the significance of this for the future of the real estate industry has been largely lost. The fact that America is aging and that the demand for real estate will shift toward an older clientele whose needs and wants are different from the mainstream market of the past is a big piece of information for the practitioner. Similarly, the fact that immigrants are highly motivated homebuyers with different expectations about the market than native–

born Americans should prompt some behavioral shifts by real estate professionals, but has not.

It is the very rare agent or broker who has implemented a system to obtain, analyze and act on information quickly. In the past, that was all right because the business was simpler. Now conditions have changed. More and more competitors have access to the business that was once the exclusive province of the real estate professional. Those competitors are generally larger, better funded and more used to looking at markets in a longer time frame.

So it's essential that real estate practitioners and firms develop the ability to use the OODA loop. Let's look at each of the elements and see how they play out in the real estate business.

OBSERVE

The beginning of the process is to get close enough to the market to see where the important trends are coming from. Observing is a systematic accumulation of facts about the behavior of those who make up your market. It involves looking at the present reality and the potential futures of your marketplace in a way that will allow you to make basic strategic decisions about how you can best capitalize on that marketplace.

That sounds very academic, but it sets that framework for what could be some very down-to-earth activities on your part. Observing is not really that hard; it only requires that you push what you see through a clearly structured filter. Your observation of the marketplace should be divided into three groups, and looked at three ways. You need to look at your present customers, your future customers and the fringe of the market. You need to do this through formal channels, direct experience and cultural evidence.

The Groups

Your *current market* is your most direct access to wants, needs and trends. Every one of the clients and customers you deal with has a story and that story can tell volumes about where the market may be going. Real estate practitioners often waste this resource, rushing off to the next listing or sale without taking the time to "debrief" the consumer about the marketplace. We described above how a post-transaction interview can be an important tool in locking the customer in (Chapter 3). It is also an important tool in learning about where the market is going. Asking the customer questions about tastes and behavior (Why do you like this type of house? Where do you see your career going? What would your friends think about this style? Do you plan to use the house to entertain very much?) can yield useful information about where the market is going.

Eight years ago, I participated in a *Money* magazine panel on the future of the house and the housing market. One of the participants, the owner of a chain of upscale furniture stores indicated that she felt the trend toward "cocooning," using the home more as an entertainment center in lieu of going out, was real and significant. She felt it would change the demand for house types (more living space, less sleeping space) and the type of furniture people would buy. She changed her inventory and advertising to reflect this and has been successful. This is the OODA loop in action.

Today's 16-year-old will be the *future market* for real estate, the homebuyer of the next century. Scary thought, isn't it? Their tastes and preferences are being formed now and will flow through the market as the demand of the future. Knowing more about them now will help you discover the emerging market of the future. Their dreams about what they want to become can give you a great deal of information about the way in which the real estate business will be conducted in the future and what product will be demanded in the market.

The immigrant population is also your market of the future. Census statistics suggest that the typical immigrant becomes a homeowner within 15 years of arriving in the United States. The flood of immigration that has hit these shores during the Eighties and Nineties is now entering the housing market and will continue to do so for the next two decades. The cultures of these immigrants are different and will affect the shape of the real estate business and the housing market in the future.

We often learn a great deal about change by observing the *fringes* of the market. Revolutions come most often from those edges, not from the mainstream. Christianity, as an example, was created by a fringe character, Paul, who interpreted the teachings of Christ for the masses. Absent this outsider, it would have remained a small sect. Often, the most important things for your life and your business are happening just outside your field of vision. Expanding that field is a way of increasing the power of your observation.

Methods of Observation

The methods of observation are ways of getting information about the present and future markets and the fringe.

In every community, there are experts on subjects relevant to your future. Usually, they are located in colleges and universities. These constitute *formal* resources that you can tap in learning about the future. Economists, sociologists, futurists and marketing specialists are all useful in getting a handle in where your markets may be growing. Identify these resources in your market area, and pick their brains. You can do this by taking a class, reading their books and articles and seeking them out for conversations. You might even want to hire them to conduct specific market observations for you. Their business for the most part is to see what's coming and determine what it means. You would be opposed to a consumer buying or selling a house without the services of a real estate professional. Why would you think of observing the future without the services of another kind of professional?

Your own *direct experience* is a second method of observation that will yield useful information. Take a look at the recent history of your business and your firm. Talk with other real estate professionals in the market about what they see occurring with their practices. What are the trends in types of houses sold? Who's buying? Is there a shift in the type of household active in the market? How important is the immigrant population in your market? These are all questions that can lead you to a classification of your experience that can point to the direction of the market of the future. Don't underestimate its value, and by all means, don't ignore it.

Be aware of the value of *cultural evidence* in generating important observations. When you're at a newsstand, browse through magazines in areas that you are either unfamiliar with or not interested in. The articles in these magazines can give you slants on your own experience that help turn seemingly unimportant facts into valuable observations. They may also point to cultural trends that will mean something for your business. The same is true for television and radio. Want to know about the homebuyers of the next decade? Take some time and watch the TV shows aimed at the younger audience and listen to the music that makes them dance. There are clues there for your future. Want to know about immigrant buyers? Spend some time in their communities and observe their behavior.

ORIENT

Finding out about things is good, but knowing what's important and what's not is crucial. Orientation is the process of taking information, determining its significance and turning it into knowledge, i.e., making the information actionable. Without an orientation to the market, no information is useful. The process of orientation follows a number of steps.

What Observations Have I Made about the Relevant Future Environment of My Business and My Market?

The key point here is *relevant*. Global warming may be an element of the future and may be of personal significance, but has little to do with your business. (Unless, of course, you decide to specialize in oceanfront properties in Des Moines.) Sorting out relevance is difficult because it gets caught up in the noise of today.

The domestic economy is clearly relevant. Generally speaking, if the future element deals with the consumption behavior or household formation patterns of people, it's relevant to you. So are employment trends and workplace behavior (for example, telecommuting trends are vital to both licensees and builders). Political events may be of some relevance, but real estate professionals give them far too much emphasis. In a decentralized, technological world, government tends to shrink in relevance.

Other areas of the external environment (particularly technology and demographics and—increasingly—the global economy) will have a great deal of relevance to the real estate business.

What Changes or Innovations Do These Observations Point To?

Some of these changes will be major. Suppose, for example, your observation tells you that consumers in the housing market are increasingly used to electronic communications and are increasingly comfortable using electronic means to execute transactions. They buy from catalogues on the phone or over the Web and regard this as an efficient and beneficial means of fulfilling their wants. You might determine that this is significant for you and that you need to place your business on a more extensive technological base in order to meet these customers where they want to do business. That is a radical shift in your business model.

Sometimes the changes are smaller—not necessarily less difficult, just smaller. In the case of increasing numbers of immigrants in the homebuying market, an awareness of cultural norms as they affect the transaction will be key. So the change implied by this observation is increased education as to the way in which people in different countries are used to doing business.

Sometimes observation leads to innovation. If your observation of changing household patterns in your market suggests that more and more homes are being purchased by "nontraditional" households (singles, unrelated individuals, multigenerational single-headed families, etc.), you might want to partner with a local builder to create housing that suits these households, with several master suites, or wider doorways and staircases and grab bars for older or infirm individuals. This is a new role for the licensee in the real estate industry.

Where Do These Observations Suggest That the Market Is Headed, But Doesn't Know It Yet?

Tough question. Wayne Gretzky answered it by saying that he skates to where the puck is going. Sony answered it by introducing the Walkman. In other words, you answer the question by taking your observations and building stories about the future consistent with the observations. Those stories will give you insight about the wants and needs of the people who will inhabit that future. That gives you a picture of the range of possible behavior in your future market.

What Opportunities Are Present in the Potential Future That Have Not as Yet Been Identified or Seized by Others?

Clearly, there are competitors who are looking at the same future as you are. Some of them have been busy creating the innovations that will be attractive to consumers in the future. But by drawing out your observations until they produce potential futures, you can see other possibilities that will give you a market edge.

Orientation is harder than observation. To determine correctly the significance of any observation to your business and your future, you need to have full information about the realities of your organization, and in particular its capacities. In the case of Verifone, a full sharing of information gives each staff member the ability to orient information toward the ends of the company. In a real estate firm, this involves ensuring that each employee and sales associate is aware of the goals of the company and empowered to share information as it is relevant to the fulfillment of those goals.

DECIDE

The decision part of the OODA loop involves the ability to analyze observations and their relevance and then choose the best method of exploiting the opportunity presented. All effective decision processes have one major characteristic: decisions are made on the most appropriate level. In the case of Verifone, the initiation of a project may take place at the level of the CEO, but the exact implementation will be in the hands of those lower in the organization. The reasoning here is simple: give control to those with the most knowledge and accountability for the result.

The best decision processes are also clean. The consultative process may be extensive, and it should be if there is a commitment to observation and orientation. In that case everyone has a piece of the truth and the puzzle is more complete when more pieces are on the board. But there is no ambiguity about scope of initiative and responsibility. You know whose decision it is and who is responsible for the success or failure of the operation.

Relatively few real estate practitioners or even real estate firms have the systems in place to convert insight to action. The decision processes are focused on short-term questions that absolutely require answers if the next transaction is to go through. In firms like Verifone, the complete orientation to the next thing in the market makes the decision process easy and direct. In the real estate business, being that far ahead of the market has a technical term: bankruptcy.

The question for real estate firms is how to integrate a decision mechanism without losing the crucial focus on today.

This is hardest for the *agent* if only because there is no one else to help. It might help here to confine the decision process to single areas at a time: decisions about how to deal with the changing client base first, then tools and techniques, etc. Using the OODA loop to improve your business then becomes a sequential process with the priorities developed during the orientation phase.

Top producers tend to have one or more personal assistants who execute different parts of the transaction. One of these can be given the responsibility of tending the OODA loop and setting up the decision making process for the agent. In other words, one of the assistants becomes the resident futurist. The skills necessary to do this job are far different from those required in the real estate transaction, so the choice of this individual should be involve identifying the research and thinking skills needed for the maintenance of the OODA loop.

For the *real estate firm,* the stakes in the decision process are higher than for any individual practitioner. Any decision made on a company-wide basis will involve the commitment of substantial resources, including capital, and run the risk of alienating the independent contractors on whom the firm's business depends. Under these conditions, the creation of a separate OODA unit is probably worthwhile, with the decision process reserved for the CEO or a senior management group.

The decision process is where most attempts at implementing the OODA loop fall apart. When a human first ate a lobster, there were probably a lot of others standing around to see if he died or not. Those guys went into real estate. Real estate professionals are big consumers of information. Many will also puzzle out what that information means in their businesses. But few have put into place the systems that allow for decisions to follow the understanding of meaning. To give yourself an edge in the market, carefully cultivate this part of the OODA loop.

ACT

Action closes the loop. The implementation of a decision to its end result is a scary thing, especially when the decision shapes your future and began with an observation of the market that may or may not have been relevant to your future. Action requires a careful consideration of time phasing. If the action is significant, like a movement to a fully automated transaction system, the sequence of steps that makes up the action will have to be done exactly or the desired result will not occur. Often this means a shift of the culture of the organization as well as the actual physical change itself.

In real estate, the cultural aspects of any action are usually the keys. The business is so traditional that any change designed to address the likely future will meet with strong resistance from those in the practice, both employees and agents. The history of innovation in the business is the history of pushback and abandonment. This has been particularly true when outside companies attempted to leverage real estate with their own businesses, as when Met Life owns Century 21. Even Cendant experienced pushback when it implemented its system with its real estate companies.

Action in real estate is also difficult because of the tight regulatory structure that surrounds the industry. License law makes it very difficult to do anything without the consent of the licensee. In addition, changes to the commission structure, such as the recent Amerinet-Costco experiment, must pass through the filter of the real estate commission.

Finally, consider general rule #3. **No action taken alone is as good as that taken jointly.** When you decide what actions you need to take to prepare for the probable future, look for strategic partners. Partners will be helpful in supplying expertise, and even capital, especially if the action involves the adoption of technology. If an innovation is to succeed in real estate, it must get the buy-in from all interested parties. You will not succeed otherwise.

NOW DO IT ALL OVER AGAIN

The future never stops changing. What works today is ineffective tomorrow; yesterday's trend is tomorrow's fad. Because of that, the OODA loop never stops turning. After your decision process yields to action, that action must be evaluated against a whole new set of observations oriented toward relevance in your business.

This means that the sensing of the market that is the guts of the OODA loop never stops. Over the next years, there will be new entrants to the real estate industry, competition from other industries, changing technology and new consumers. All these have to be constantly factored into your planning process, into your OODA loop to enable you to stay ahead of the changes that will shape your future, be there ahead of the market and position yourself to be the consumer's most attractive option.

HOW CAN I USE THIS CHAPTER?

Using the OODA loop is no longer a luxury. In the competitive real estate market, it's a *necessity*. How do I do it?

- Build yourself an OODA loop. It may sound more complicated in this description than it is in reality, but in either case, it's clearly feasible for the individual or for the firm.
- Within the firm, it's easiest to create an OODA unit reporting directly to the CEO. The unit will monitor information, interpret it within the goals and pur-

poses of the firm and drive the decision process. It will bring to senior management those factors most important to its decision making process. *But it must be listened to.* Creating the OODA unit and then ignoring it is a waste of resource now and a greater waste of resources later.

- For the individual, the easiest way to get it done is to make some friends. Create an informal advisory group, preferably including some local experts from the academic community. You can tap them from time to time for observations about the future and their meaning to you. Your decisions and actions are yours alone, but it never hurts to get a diversity of opinion to guide your thinking.

Use the OODA loop to mine your bits (Chapter 6) and lock your customer in for life (Chapter 3).

Know What Business You're In

The most profitable businesses of the future will act as knowledge brokers, linking insights into what's available with insights into the consumer's individual needs and preferences.

–Robert Reich, former Secretary of Labor

POP QUIZ

Name the businesses of the following companies:

> McDonald's
> American Express
> Sara Lee
> General Motors
> Nike

If you answered fast food, travel services, pastries, automobiles and athletic shoes (alternate answer: Michael Jordan), you are a keen observer of the current scene who keeps up with the news. And you're dead wrong. McDonald's is a real estate company, American Express is a document handler, Sara Lee manages brand names, Nike is a clothing distributor and General Motors is a consumer finance company. (The last one is a little unfair since GM is still in the business of making vehicles. It just makes more profit by financing them than selling them.) Each of these companies presents a face to the world that is consistent with its major business but that masks its true purpose.

NOBODY DOESN'T LIKE SARA LEE . . . WHATEVER IT IS

About a year ago, Sara Lee, the famous maker of cakes, pies and snack foods, stopped making them. Oh, you can still go to the store and buy Sara Lee brand products, and they're fresh, but Sara Lee doesn't manufacture them. It licensed its brand to a number of independent producers who create the product and market it under the Sara Lee name.

What does Sara Lee do? It manages the brand name. It sees that quality control is maintained, original recipes are used and the name is promoted. The reasoning behind the switch is quite simple. The brand name is the most valuable asset that Sara Lee possesses. It has no particular market advantage in the production of cake; any one of a hundred companies can do it as well. So why not get rid of all the overhead and production headaches and just leverage the brand? This is the path it has chosen, and Sara Lee is now solely a brand management company.

In making this change, it joins a number of other companies who have similarly gotten out of the manufacturing business and into brand management. Nike is a very high profile case in point. All Nike products are manufactured by independent companies mostly located offshore. Nike itself distributes these products and promotes the brand name. Most of its budget is devoted to promotion. And they do it quite well, as anyone who's ever watched sports on television can tell you.

DID SOMEBODY SAY REAL ESTATE DEVELOPER?

McDonald's is not in the fast food business. McDonald's is a real estate company. It owns parcels of land throughout the country, patents and trademarks on food products, and the licensing rights to a brand name. It combines the three in order to maximize the value of its real estate.

When you go into a McDonald's store (I hesitate to call them restaurants), the sights, sounds and smells will be quite familiar. It is this familiarity that draws customers back over and over. The sensory package that McDonald's offers you varies little from store to store, regardless of the location. That consistency that makes the brand is achieved through the rigorous training of the franchisee, who is probably a graduate of "Hamburger University," the McDonald's training facility in suburban Chicago. There, every procedure of McDonald's operations is taught to the point where the franchisee will be able to rigorously train his own staff.

The result is that operating a McDonald's is profitable to the franchisee. McDonald's has created a system that will maximize the revenue from each square foot of each parcel of land that it owns and on which it grants a franchise to run a store. McDonald's took food service technology and franchised it, reinventing themselves as a real estate company, owning ground leases and using advertising to drive people through their real estate.

KNOW WHAT YOU DO

This last rule is not really new. It's an evergreen rule that takes on added significance in a technocentric world. We don't fly on Union Pacific Airlines. The reason is that at the turn of the Twentieth Century, Union Pacific defined its business as railroads. So, several years later, it took no notice of the experiments taking place on the North Carolina coast. If it had consciously been in the business of transporting people and things (which of course it was) then it could possibly have incorporated the Wright Brothers into its business development division.

There are more modern examples as well. American Express originated as a company that transported valuables and gradually evolved into the travel service giant known to the public. But about twenty years ago, it rediscovered its identity as a document delivery and financial services business. Through mergers and acquisitions (it was on both sides), it has been able to stay focussed on its business yet change its entire delivery system.

There are examples, too, of companies that don't know what they do and suffer for it. Go into any school system in the United States and ask the superintendent what business he's in. He'll tell you that his business is education, and then wax eloquent about how the system is improving the educational experience of our most treasured possession, our youth, etc.

That might well be the mission of the system (and it should be) and the school principals, but the superintendent is running a business. It has a budget significant in size for his jurisdiction, it is a major employer, and it is a key part of the local infrastructure. Yet most school districts derive their leadership from classroom veterans, and most are (mentally) still in the classroom. It shows. Overstaffing, dated technology and just plain waste plague virtually every public school system in the United States. It's interesting that several large districts have hired superintendents whose background is primarily business. Perhaps they're waking up to what their real business is.

Closer to home, the RIN experiment as originally executed by the National Association of REALTORS® was a classic case of not being conscious of what business you're in. The original RIN concept, creating an electronic connectivity that would enable REALTORS® exclusive access to the information that fueled the transaction, was designed to keep the REALTOR® as the center of the transaction.

So far, so good. But NAR tried to accomplish this in-house, a task that required competencies it didn't possess. It tried to buy them; it didn't work. *It is exceptionally hard to acquire competencies you don't have to the degree you need them to excel in the market.* The highly successful successor to RIN, Real Select, works because it's a partnership that weds two vital and complementary but separate competencies, knowledge of the real estate industry and technological expertise (see Chapter 5).

FIGURING IT OUT

Okay, how do I figure out what my business is? Or, since real estate is essentially a small business industry, what are my core business competencies? To put it another way, what is it that I do that people will willingly pay me for? The process of identifying your core business is like peeling an onion (with more tears). You look at what you do and then proceed to ask why you do that until you get to the point of revealing what the customer really values in what you offer.

To start, with, real estate has about as much to do with houses and land as McDonald's does with hamburgers and fries. These are the reasons the *consumer* uses the service of the real estate professional. In reality, the real estate professional is not in the business of buying and selling real estate, but rather *brokering information* about real estate.

So real estate is an information business (how many times have we said that!). The information may be simple—what's on the market?—or it may be complex—the real reasons why this particular house has been on the market for 16 months. The essence of the business is information. It's why the public comes and it's what generates compensation for the licensee. The real estate professional got paid for being the gatekeeper and opening the door to all the other parts of the real estate transaction.

But information is now automated. In a world dominated by bits and the power of one, anybody can access the information of what's available in the market and rearrange it in any set of categories he wants. Customization of information is cheap and easy. Anyone can do it and everyone will. The result will be as satisfying to the consumer as if it came from the biggest real estate company in the country. This removes the rewards for simply possessing information. The core business can't be information. At least, it can't be information if you expect to make a profit.

So where's the core business? It's *knowledge*–the creation of packages of information (bits, not atoms) that are of value to consumers because they are actionable. Information about the physical dimensions, location and price of a house is easy to get. That the house is in an area that has been rezoned commercial and the lovely, tree-shaded two–lane road it sits on is about to be widened to six lanes are invaluable pieces of knowledge. Mortgage loans and terms offered in the market can be found on the Internet; having someone explain the details and the ramifications of each loan type for now and the future is a valuable service.

THE CORE BUSINESS COMPETENCIES

But is it really knowledge that the consumer seeks and values? In part it is, but the real estate professional goes further.

During the buying or selling process, the licensee becomes a *guide and counselor* to the consumer. Especially now in the era of buyer agency, the real estate practitioner becomes the counselor to the household, advising not only on the specifics of the property but also on the way in which the property is best presented for sale and the way the property will fit their long-term goals.

The licensee also becomes the *negotiator* for the household, obtaining the best possible terms for the purchase or sale. This is a skill that most consumers do not feel they possess and will gladly pay for someone to supply it.

Throughout the process, the real estate professional is the *transaction manager,* assuring that in the end a transaction that suits the needs of the client will be consummated. Think of the general contractor in the remodeling of a house. Assuring everything that must be done is done in the proper sequence at the least cost is a valuable contribution to the customer.

The interesting commonality here is that these are all people skills that are difficult to replicate by technology. At least for now. (Eventually—meaning in about ten years—expert systems and artificial intelligence will make the best people skills of the best real estate people available to anyone through software.)

The roles of counselor, negotiator and manager constitute the core business of any licensee. Regardless of what happens to the business model of the real estate industry or the degree to which portions of the transactions are automated, the wisdom and counsel of someone familiar with and experienced in the real estate market will provide that value-added.

Notice that nothing in this description referred to the hauling around of papers or people. Nothing referenced the MLS or owning information. All that is superfluous to the real business of real estate. When the McDonald brothers and Ray Kroc teamed up in the Fifties, they fried hamburgers on stoves that were primitive by today's automation standards. Yet, the business has not changed. The things we worry about today are simply the tools we now use. They are the rotary-dial telephones of the future.

PUTTING IT ALL TOGETHER

Today's consumer wants a real estate transaction that's better, faster and cheaper. She knows that a good portion of what's needed can be done easily and virtually cost-free by using the Internet. She knows that she's found the dream house and wants to get in as quickly as possible. She also knows that searching a database and printing out information derived from certain criteria is not worth the high rates the real estate practitioner is charging.

When you combine consumer expectations with the essential business of the real estate industry in providing knowledge for the consumer, the final piece of the puzzle appears. The real estate business is about creating a channel that will provide the same satisfying and beneficial experience for every customer every time he or she uses that agent or that firm. That will be the brand of the real estate business.

How do you do it? Throughout the book, I've described bits and pieces of the model that can be used to practice the essential business of real estate. It involves using the licensee in the three key roles—counselor, negotiator, manager—described above and turning the rest of the transaction over to a clerical employee to execute electronically. This may seem to be a major cultural shift for the real estate industry. After all, doesn't the agent have full control over every aspect of the consumer's transaction?

The reality is that the perception of value received on the part of the consumer and the perception of value delivered by the licensee diverge. The consumer values sound advice and a transaction that happens immediately (in the words of Jean-Luc Picard, "Make it so, number one"). The agent sees value in time put in and tasks accomplished. In the face of this discrepancy, who's right? The customer is right, of course.

If the licensee or the firm focuses on the real business of real estate as we've defined it above, the extraneous stuff falls away, even when it seemed that this stuff was the core of the business. One of the popular phrases in the industry—one that is shorthand for meeting the new competitors in the market—is "Keep the REALTOR® at the center of the transaction." I would propose that this be turned around to say, "Keep the consumer at the center of the transaction." When this is done, the real estate business will have no trouble at all understanding what business it's in.

DO I HAVE TO?

The old question pops up again here. I'm doing so well in this great economy. I've got ten years and then I'll retire. Do I have to figure out what business I'm in and change the way I do things? No, you don't, but if you fail to plan, you plan to fail. The world is changing far too quickly to allow anyone to stand pat. What works today will be tomorrow's relic. Already the real estate business has changed because of the spread of information. As consumers get faster, better and cheaper goods and services anywhere, they'll expect them everywhere.

You ignore this at your own peril. Your business (as you conceived of it) is being invaded by mortgage bankers, title companies, software providers and financial institutions. They are bigger, better capitalized and more technologically advanced. More importantly, they are entering with a new model that is automated and consumer-centric. If you don't capitalize on your advantages, they will drive you out of business.

Fortunately, there are significant advantages present in the real estate business. The biggest is trust from the general public. They are accustomed to going to the real estate professional as the first stop in the home transaction process.

They are accustomed to relying on the real estate professional for advice and counsel. They are accustomed to engaging in a real estate process managed by the real estate professional. *And no one has shown them a different or better process yet.* The advantage of the real estate business is credibility in introducing the new process.

EXPANDING THE MARKET FOR YOUR TALENTS

Understanding your core business competencies is important in planning your future. It is entirely possible that the real estate business will shift to become dominated by large firms using a corporate model and employees. It is still possible to use your core competencies in other areas without changing what you do very much. In an organization, this is being true to the core purpose. For example, Disney's core purpose is making people happy. The history of the company has been the application of that core purpose to different business lines. If you know what business you're in, you can shift among business lines without a great deal of strain.

Right now, there is a clear opportunity in the realization that the core business competencies of the real estate professional are counseling, negotiation and management. In Chapter 1, we discussed the impact that an aging population will have on the real estate business. This is combining with the buoyant stock market to have an even greater impact on a somewhat related business, financial planning.

The aging of the baby boom is creating a generation obsessed with educating its children and crafting a prosperous retirement. Over the next quarter century, the over-55 population will increase by about 38 million people (see Figure 9.1). More importantly, those that make it to age 65 without a chronic or debilitating illness can expect to live

FIGURE 9.1   Household Projection 1995 to 2010

Household Projection
1995 to 2010

Age of Head of Household

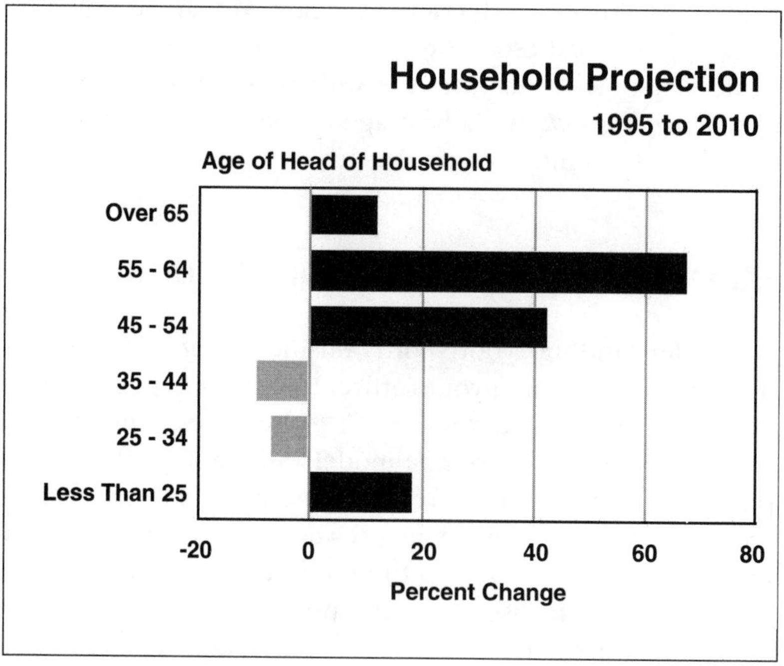

Source: John Tuccillo

another 25 years. During that time, it's likely that medical breakthroughs will add another decade to the life span. Add to this the financial uncertainty of Social Security and the result is a significant group of people who are very concerned about making their resources stretch over longer and longer periods.

The surging stock market and, in some places, rising real estate values, have created a new class of wealth in the United States. The prevalence of pension and 401(k) plans, as well as expanded access to Individual Retirement Accounts, has increased the wealth of even average Americans. By 1997, stock and bond holdings exceeded home equity in household portfolios. A large number of these households have no family history of being wealthy nor do they have any source of reliable advice outside of the company human resource specialist who administers the pension plan. They know about the value of planning and its use in maximizing their wealth and using it to satisfy the household's goals, because they read *Money* magazine and watch CNBC and CNN.

The financial planning profession has its hands full with the upper-income clients they have traditionally served and have chosen not to compete for middle-class financial planning business. In their absence, banks, insurance companies and other financial services companies have begun to advertise their ability to serve this market.

COUNSELING AND MANAGING = COUNSELING AND MANAGING

Can real estate professionals enter the field? Should they? At its heart, financial planning requires knowledge of investments and a gift for counseling. Does that answer the question? It's a short step from counseling a prospective buyer and seller about their biggest purchase ever to helping a household plan its portfolio to meet its long-term goals. It's also a short step from working with a team of appraisers, mortgage lenders, title companies and attorneys to make a home transaction work to working with a team of accountants and tax attorneys to help build a secure future for a baby boomer household.

There's another reason for considering using your core competencies in the planning area. Over the past decade (roughly since the Tax Act of 1986 became effective) home equity has become as liquid as any other asset in the portfolio. Refinancing and borrowing against equity are easier and cheaper (because of technology). The ability to prepay the mortgage through additional payments to principal without penalty has become a regular part of the landscape. So households can add or subtract home equity in their portfolio as easily as deposits and withdrawals from a savings account.

The real estate professional knows more about the housing and housing finance markets than any other professional involved with household wealth. She is the prime source of advice about the proper role of the housing asset in the overall planning of the household. Do housing appreciation rates in the area indicate that reducing equity in the house and investing in the stock market is the wise move? Should home equity be counted on as a supplementary retirement fund or a college savings account or not? These are questions that are key to the planning process for most middle class households. No one is better positioned to give the right answers. And despite the self-image of the real estate professional, few are more trusted by households.

POSITIONING IS EVERYTHING

Of course, none of this is possible without a clear idea of what your core business competencies are. If you define your business as relaying property information from buyers to sellers and bringing them together to do a deal, then that's what you'll do until Microsoft or CityPlace or someone else takes the market. But if you focus clearly on counseling, negotiating and managing as your key competencies, then they can be applied in a variety of complementary business lines.

Here's where positioning comes in. Your business processes must reflect your core business competencies. That means getting rid of the trivia that locks you into the old system of real estate and only real estate. Delegating extraneous functions to clerks or machines (or better yet, clerks operating machines) allows you to use your core competencies in their (not to coin a phrase) highest and best uses.

In real estate that means creating the transaction experience for the consumer that will create value by making it happen faster, better and cheaper. Remember that the greatest costs to the consumer of buying and selling a home are time and stress. The current system is cumbersome in that it takes large quantities of time and generates high stress. So the process is costly and distasteful for the average consumer. To the extent that you can create a system that will give the consumer back time and take away stress, you have created value that cannot be competed away. If at the same time you deliver your core competencies of counseling, negotiation and management, you've doubled the value delivered in the marketplace.

Beyond real estate, there are other business lines that will successfully use the core competencies that are possessed by real estate professionals. The financial planning example is the one that comes most readily to mind, but almost any market application could use these competencies. You don't know where your core competencies will lead you, but following them is not a bad idea; look at the story of Laura Herring (see Chapter 2).

HOW CAN I USE THIS CHAPTER?

Understanding your core business competencies is crucial in a world where change is endemic and competition is coming from all sides. Following the same old path may help you ride out this business cycle, but it won't get you much further. The consumer is getting better, faster and cheaper service from a raft of manufacturing and service industries. Real estate cannot hold itself out as an exception to that trend.

- Getting there from here is not complicated, but neither is it easy. It will require a reassessment of what you do and how you do it.
- Make an assessment of how you spend your time. How much of it is related to the core business competencies—counseling, negotiation and management? It should be the majority of your effort.
- Analyze your business processes. Do they allow you to concentrate on exercising your core competencies or do they trap you in extraneous activity?
- Design a business system that delivers to the consumer a satisfying and consistent transaction experience every time. Make it as automated as possible, and use your time to give that consumer the extra helping of value that comes from your core business competencies.
- Build into your practice or organization the flexibility to use your core competencies by organizing around the competencies.
- Take some time and plan how you can best use your core competencies to develop a competitive edge in other business lines. Look for strategic partners to supplement and complement your competencies. Remember, it's very difficult to develop or buy core competencies to the degree to which you will need them to excel in the market.

Listen to your customers. They will be the best source of insight as to how your core business competencies can be employed to deliver value to the market.

When you have clarified the business you're in, you can create an OODA loop (Chapter 8) to build market insight and position. You will also create an experience (Chapter 7) that will deliver value to the market and be able to lock your customer in for life (Chapter 3).

Playing by the Rules

Your company's software consists of your innovative people, your corporate culture, your collective capacity for generating, evaluating, accepting and implementing new thought.[1]

    –Don Peppers and Martha Rogers,
    The One to One Future, p. 390

A QUICK REVIEW

In case you haven't been paying attention, here are the rules again:

The General Rules

- Your business is global, whether or not you sell beyond the boundaries of your town.
- Speed is everything.
- You'll never walk alone. Business is done, and has been since before GM linked up with Nissan to create the Saturn, through strategic alliances.
- Abandon your successes quickly.

The Specific Rules:

Rule #1: **The most powerful economic unit is the individual.**

Rule #2: **Lock the customer in for life by creating unique value.**

---

[1] From *The One to One Future* by Don Peppers and Martha Rogers, Ph.D. Copyright ©1993 by Don Peppers and Martha Rogers, Ph.D. Used by permission of Doubleday, a division of Random House, Inc.

Rule #3: **The middle is disappearing.**
Rule #4: **Think content.**
Rule #5: **Mine your bits.**
Rule #6: **Sell the experience, not the product.**
Rule #7: **Feed the OODA loop.**
Rule #8: **Know What Business You're In.**

THE RULES APPLY TO EVERYONE EQUALLY

You can't escape them. These rules are derived from the environment surrounding not only the real estate business but also the economy and business in general. The changes that occurred because of how technology has affected the flow and reach of information have forever altered the way in which business is done and who can do it. A little later we talk about the specific competencies that will be needed to apply the rules to the best possible advantage. For now, let's just say that what served you best in the past may have no impact on success in the future.

If you do not move toward implementing these rules, then your ability to compete for the next decade is gone. Either your own competitors in the real estate business will adopt them and take your market, or some firm from outside the real estate industry that already plays by the rules will enter the business and immediately take market share. The question for you is not "if" but "when."

Adapting the rules to your business will require three things:

1. **Capital.** The real estate business has traditionally been free of barriers to entry, particularly in the area of capital. The production process for real estate services was centered on people, not machinery. Rent for space, some office equipment and supplies, signage and a few other items were all the capital

needed. But with the revolution in information technology, the cost of doing business has gone up. Creating a system that consistently delivers consumer satisfaction will require integrated technology. This is done only through the acquisition of a substantial amount of capital in the form of hardware and software.

2. **The system.** The thrust of the rules is the use of technology to put together a system that produces customer satisfaction in the same way every time. In short, the rules will help you establish and leverage a brand name. The system relies heavily on automating information flow in a fast, easy manner, while using skilled professionals to use knowledge to create consumer value.

3. **People.** Using an integrated system requires a new role for the workforce in real estate. Your agents will need to adjust to a role that uses only their professional talents. They will no longer be charged with running documents all over town or phoning to create appointments. Conversely, they will be called upon to fit a package of services more specifically to a given customer or client. How do you harness the intelligence of your labor force? This is especially a problem for REALTORS® because of the independent contractor status. On top of this, you will need to increase the number of your salaried employees, since the system will require more clerical functions.

These three factors, combined as the rules dictate they should, create a new look for the real estate industry. The business is not now, for the most part, done this way. **The major gap is the use of the system.** And that's the most difficult piece of the puzzle. Capital can be acquired and people can be retrained. Most firms have logos, forms and certain office routines. They do not have systems.

There is one segment of the business where some of the rules have been adopted. Top producers have generally built their successes on the foundation of a business system that delivers customer satisfaction every time. Most have done this through the use of assistants divided along functional lines: some list, some carry documents, some oversee the settlement process, etc. In other words, they handle the repetitive tasks that are nearly the same in every transaction. In some cases, the assistants are unlicensed and in more cases they're salaried.

The result is that the super-agent can concentrate on addressing the specific needs of clients—the needs that differ from transaction to transaction. But even the top producer systems fall short of playing by the rules in two ways. First, few of them mine their bits. Data analysis has no obvious payoff, so it's often neglected. Second, the system is predicated on the use of labor, not automation. Ultimately, the best systems will be people-proof, centered around technology and automatic.

So it's not impossible to develop a consistent system. On the firm level, the task is harder because of the lack of control by the broker over the licensees associated with her firm. It also requires a greater investment, mainly in enough supporting hardware and software. It also requires more management, including managers who can deal with clerical, salaried employees.

THE RULES DON'T APPLY TO EVERYONE EQUALLY

The rules are like musk cologne. They come out of the bottle smelling the same, but once they hit the skin they take on a unique odor. The element that makes the application of the rules unique to each individual or firm is culture, the sum of all the personalities, history and relationships that make up the firm or the practice.

*A*ny organization, be it a tribe or a company, builds up "endotruths" and "exotruths" about itself. Endotruths are the ones known inside but not outside the microculture, the ones that drive deep to its beginnings and shape the internal understanding. Exotruths are the presumed truths about the tribe, the ones that determine the external value and reputation and that cannot be shaken loose even by denying them. Collectively, the two truths explain why two organizations—the Army and the Marines, the *Chicago Tribune* and the *Miami Herald,* the American Cancer Society and the American Heart Association—can be in fundamentally the same business and yet have radically different cultures and be understood from outside in radically different ways. Tribes stamp us from within and without.[1]

[1] Jim Taylor and Watts Wacker, *The Five Hundred Year Delta,* Harper Business, 1997, p. 203.

It is impossible to ignore culture. It shapes what we do, how we relate to each other, and how business gets done. It determines the way you treat your agents, employees and assistants. It dictates how you deal with customers, the way you communicate with them and your ultimate relationship with them.

The manner in which you adopt the new rules will depend a great deal on your culture. Take as an example an organization that relies heavily on highly productive older agents who have been with the company for a long time. In that case, the culture of the company is likely to be dominated by the agents, and less accepting of technology. The rules can be implemented, but with an emphasis on relationship building. Technological change in that case will have to be packaged in terms of easy-to-use tools that relate closely to the habits of the agents.

Before you implement the rules, you need to do a cultural assessment of your firm or your practice. Examine your operation in the following dimensions:

Demographics

Draw an age, experience and longevity profile of your personnel. Generally (although not always) more age and experience and lower turnover signify a stronger culture and one that is more people oriented than technological. The rules are harder to implement directly with this profile. Don't weight everyone equally. Overemphasize the most valuable personnel—those who have the most to offer in positioning the practice for the future.

Leadership

Determine who makes decisions in the organization. Where decision-making is centralized (as is often the case with older, founder-led firms), implementation of the rules is easier than when decisions are made by a large group of people. By the way, the decisions that need to be scrutinized include those that affect the flow of business. So, the color of the logo is less important than who schedules advertising and who controls the transaction.

Cohesion

The ends of this spectrum are easy to define. On one end, the firm has a clear identity to which the agents relate closely. The polar opposite is the body shop that moves people in and out because production is associated with "feet on the street." Where does your firm lie? In the first case, conversion to the new rules is easier because the trust level will allow you to lead the way to change.

Management

Playing by the rules requires a coordinated management team to lead and implement change. Is your management team focused? Does it have a common vision? Does it command the respect of your personnel? It is crucial that your culture recognizes clear authority and direction.

CULTURE AND THE RULES

Culture affects *how* you implement the rules, not whether you do. Any organization with an identity can use the rules to enter the knowledge economy in an effective way. Clearly, however, the order in which you adopt the rules and the methods you use must be consistent with the culture of your organization.

The most applicable of the rules to any organization is the OODA loop. No organization can afford to ignore the events of the market or the need to react to them quickly. In the real estate industry, the OODA process is most effectively accomplished without the use of technology. But it requires a dedication to sharing knowledge within the organization instantly and freely. Without strong cultural cohesion, using this rule will be very difficult.

In contrast, mining your bits is perhaps the most difficult of all the rules. It requires a strong commitment to technology and an experienced and dependable front office staff. It will also entail education of your agents in how to access and use the assembled databases in their listing and selling activities. Your culture must exhibit a high degree of cohesion and managerial control. Almost as important, your associates should be younger and inexperienced; then they will be more receptive to the use of a technology–intensive delivery system.

These represent the extremes of the rules. If we designate them Culture #1 and Culture #2, we can classify the rules as being easier or harder to implement. The ease or difficulty of implementation refers to the compatibility of the culture with the major thrust of the rule. Remember, all the rules can be implemented in either type of culture. But how you implement the rules must conform to your culture.

Culture and the Rules: Ease of Implementation

Culture #1	*Culture #2*
Know The Business You're In	Sell the Experience
The Power of One	Lock the Customer In
Feed the OODA Loop	Mine Your Bits
The Middle Is Disappearing	Think Content

CHANGING CULTURE

Suppose that you want to change your culture. Is it possible to remake the organization in such a way that the rules are easier to implement? The answer is, yes, with difficulty. For most real estate organizations, cultural change implies personnel change. Since the major input to the real estate services production process is the agent, those agents will determine the prevailing culture.

But implementing the rules may best be done by changing people. Ultimately, doing business in the new environment means substituting machines for people. Some elements of the settlement process (property descriptions, mortgages) are already online. The rest (appraisals, title information, and electronic signature verification) is coming soon. Even the efficient systems of top producers will evolve from relying on people to using machines. More importantly, the "feet on the street" strategy that has been customary in the business will no longer work. The numbers of agents who are not making even the minimum wage are large. (Statistics from NAR suggest that this could be as much as half the salespeople in the industry).

This group represents a prime opportunity for both cultural change and rule implementation. To implement the rules, you will need to switch to a system that uses salaried personnel to manage the transaction and reserve the use of (fewer) professionals to do the counseling and negotiating they can do well. This can be done by converting low-producing agents into the salaried labor force that can implement the automated systems suggested by the rules.

PERSONAL CHANGE

For individuals, playing by the rules will mean making some changes as well. One of the first things involved in any change is making an inventory of competencies and stacking them up against the competencies needed to accomplish the change. If you have been successful in real estate, you have developed the tools to continue that success. As the market shifts, some of those tools will no longer lead to that success; others will have to replace them.

One talent that will not change in the new environment is the need to understand and relate to people. In fact, that becomes more important as consumers are better able to decide upon and articulate their needs. But this is a new and different breed of consumer. The difference is that the consumer now expects more and better service. Part of this is due to the dominance of the baby-boom generation. They are older, richer and pickier than previous generations. Part is the way information has increased the power of one. (The hallmark of the baby boomers has been certainty over what's right for them and what's right for you, coupled with a penchant for telling everyone what they should do. Armed with more information, courtesy of the Internet, they are the customers from hell.)

So the relationship with the customer must be more personalized. Rather than attempting to put the consumer through a set list of processes, the professional will need to probe more deeply into the specific needs of each customer, and then create a package of services targeted directly to those needs. Being a pal is attractive, but offering real value is better. The successful real estate practitioner will always need to be a strong people specialist, but the way that competency works out in practice will differ in the future.

. . . AND MORE CHANGES

There are other competencies that the new rules dictate that may not have been present in the successes of the past.

Understanding of Technology

Regardless of your culture, now or in the future, you will need to be comfortable with technology. Real estate professionals have grown into everything from fax machines to cell phones; they will soon grow into wireless modems and Internet marketing. Those who don't have the ability to keep up with developments in information technology and understand how these developments can help their businesses will fall behind in the market of the future.

Doing this requires input and time. The input can come from the regular reading of magazines like *Wired* that make current technology accessible and readable. The time involved is your own reflection on the meaning of what you have discovered. It's really a variation of the OODA loop.

Creation of Knowledge

Information is the currency of the past; knowledge is the currency of the future. You need to fill up your bank account. Playing by the rules means the ability to take information and make it actionable for the consumer. This requires an understanding of where information is, how to access it and how to combine it to meet consumer needs.

This competency is best acquired through strategic partnerships. Your ability is probably highest in ascertaining what the needs, wants and motivation of the consumer are. You will also know where information can be found. Someone with a technical specialty will be most familiar with collateral and relational databases and be able to combine them to help you answer your client's needs.

Market Foresight

The rules work best when you combine them with knowledge of where your market will be going. Economic conditions are important, but they are primarily short term in nature. The longest stretch of expansion or contraction in the postwar economy has only lasted seven years. Against a 25-year future, that's not much. More important is a reading of the longer-term trends. Is the employment base of your market area shifting in significant ways? Is technology changing the way people live and work in your market area? How are the demographics of your market period changing? Are aging or immigration significant factors?

Market foresight is a product of dedication and discipline. Set aside some thinking and reading time to look at trends as they shape up in your market. Look at magazines like *The Futurist* and *American Demographics* to figure out what's happening nationally and internationally. Visit with a local expert from a university or consulting firm to get a feel for the specifics of your market. And then keep doing it.

A FINAL WORD

The rules I've laid out in this book seem to me to be the keys to succeeding in the consumer-centric, technologically savvy world of the future. If you follow them, you will be creating the real estate practice of the future. The problem is that the rate of change is unpredictable so the rate of implementing the rules is uncertain as well.

Attempting to move ahead of the market into the future has historically been a recipe for failure in real estate. It is an imitative business that will adopt innovation only after it has proven profitable. Jumping to the new rules will put you out on a limb with no assurance that you're in the right tree. It's a gamble. But we are all serious gamblers. We gamble on the future in all of our personal and business decisions and the stakes are high. Playing by the new rules may well shorten your odds.

BIBLIOGRAPHY

Your First Strategic Partners: A Short Bibliography

The following books all deal with one or more aspects of business strategy in the information age. They are accessible to the lay reader and will help you understand better the way the new rules play out in this market. Pick up one or two of them and read them through.

Michael H. Annison, *Managing the Whirlwind,* MGMA, 1993. One of the best summaries of the kind of turmoil that the information age plunges us into.

Roger D. Blackwell, *From Mind to Market,* Harper Business, 1997. A new approach to marketing that focuses on how to bring the customer into the marketing loop. And Blackwell is the son of a REALTOR®.

Daniel Burrus, with Roger Gittines, *Technotrends,* Harper Business, 1993. The best book on how to use the new technologies to accomplish your end. It's told in almost novel-style, and very well written.

Charles Handy, *The Age of Paradox,* Harvard Business School Press, 1994. Handy is an Irish philosopher who has an interesting handle on the underlying forces that make the modern market tick.

Nicholas Imperato and Oren Harari, *Jumping the Curve,* Jossey-Bass, 1994. Sometimes the future is best reached by large moves rather than small. This book shows the way to make the strategic jumps that may be necessary.

Nicholas Negroponte, *Being Digital,* Knopf, 1995. A classic work that explains the technical detail of the information technology in a way we can all understand. Negroponte is a regular columnist for *WiReD* magazine, another worthwhile read.

Don Peppers and Martha Rogers, *The One to One Future,* Doubleday, 1993. The marketing book for the information age. The marketing stories discussed make the book worthwhile. But there's much more.

Don Tapscott, *The Digital Economy,* McGraw-Hill, 1996. The major focus here is the way in which technology affects the information business itself. It has a great discussion of the disappearing middle.

Jim Taylor and Watts Wacker, *The 500 Year Delta,* Harper Business, 1997. This book is an imaginative view of the age we live in and will produce some real insight in how to best explore it. Think of it as a cross between futurism and business strategy.

INDEX